First Human-Centered Large Language Modeling Workshop (HuCLLM 2024)

Bangkok, Thailand
15 August 2024

ISBN: 979-8-3313-0164-4

Printed from e-media with permission by:

Curran Associates, Inc.
57 Morehouse Lane
Red Hook, NY 12571

Some format issues inherent in the e-media version may also appear in this print version.

Printed with permission by Curran Associates, Inc. (2025)

Association for Computational Linguistics
209 N. Eighth Street
Stroudsburg, Pennsylvania 18360

Phone: 1-570-476-8006
Fax: 1-570-476-0860

acl@aclweb.org

Additional copies of this publication are available from:

Curran Associates, Inc.
57 Morehouse Lane
Red Hook, NY 12571 USA
Phone: 845-758-0400
Fax: 845-758-2633
Email: curran@proceedings.com
Web: www.proceedings.com

HuCLLM 2024

The First Human-Centered Large Language Modeling Workshop

Proceedings of the Workshop

August 15, 2024

Association for Computational Linguistics (ACL)
317 Sidney Baker St. S
Suite 400 - 134
Kerrville, TX 78028
USA
Tel: +1-855-225-1962
acl@aclweb.org

Introduction

A word's meaning resides in the heart and soul of its "generator" - people. How do we include human (personal, social, cultural, situational) context, ethically, into LLMs – the base models of our NLP systems?

Language modeling in the context of its source [author] and target [audience] can enable NLP systems to better understand human language. Advances in *human-centered NLP* have established the importance of modeling the human context holistically, including personal, social, cultural, and situational factors in NLP systems. Yet, our NLP systems have become heavily reliant on large language models that do not capture the human context.

Human language is highly dependent on the rich and complex human context such as (a) *who* is speaking, (b) to *whom*, (c) *where* (situation/environment) and (d) *when* (time and place). It is additionally moderated by the changing human states of being such as their mental and emotional states.

Current large language models can possibly simulate some form of human context given their large scale of parameters and pre-training data. However, they do not explicitly process language in the higher order structure of language – connecting documents to people, the "source" of the language.

Prior work has demonstrated the benefits of including the author's information using LLMs for downstream NLP tasks. Recent research has also shown that LLMs can benefit from including additional author context in the LM pre-training task itself. Progress in the direction of merging the two successful parallels, i.e., human-centered NLP and LLMs, drives us toward creating a vision of human-centered LLMs for the future of NLP in the era of LLMs.

Human-centered large language modeling has the potential to bring promising improvements in human-centric applications through multiple domains such as healthcare, education, consumerism, etc. Simultaneously, this new research focus also brings multitudes of unexplored architectural, data, technical, fairness, and ethical challenges. With our first edition of the Human-Centered Large Language Modeling (HuCLLM) workshop, we aim to create a platform where researchers can present rising challenges and solutions in building human-centered NLP models that bring together the ideas of human and social factors adaptation into the base LLMs of our NLP systems.

We received 35 submissions, of which 18 were accepted for presentation at the workshop. These papers will be presented at oral and poster sessions on the day of the workshop. The workshop day will also include keynote talks and a panel session on human-centered large language modeling. We thank all our participants and reviewers for their work. We hope you enjoy the first edition of HuCLLM and the research published in these proceedings.

Nikita Soni, Lucie Flek, Ashish Sharma, Diyi Yang, Sara Hooker, H Andrew Schwartz

HuCLLM 2024 Chairs

Acknowledgements This workshop is supported in part by the Office of the Director of National Intelligence (ODNI), Intelligence Advanced Research Projects Activity (IARPA), via the HIATUS Program contract 2022-22072200005, and LAMARR Institute for Machine Learning and Artificial Intelligence. The views and conclusions contained herein are those of the authors and should not be interpreted as necessarily representing the official policies, either expressed or implied, of ODNI, IARPA, or the U.S. Government. The U.S. Government is authorized to reproduce and distribute reprints for governmental purposes notwithstanding any copyright annotation therein.

Organizing Committee

Workshop Organizers

Nikita Soni, Stony Brook University
Lucie Flek, University of Bonn
Ashish Sharma, University of Washington
Diyi Yang, Stanford University
Sara Hooker, Cohere For AI
H. Andrew Schwartz, Stony Brook University

Program Committee

Emergency Reviewers

Dana Moukheiber, Massachusetts Institute of Technology

Program Committee

Gavin Abercrombie, Heriot-Watt University
Maria Antoniak, Allen Institute for AI
Shaina Ashraf, Math and CS, Marburg University and Rheinische Friedrich-Wilhelms Universität Bonn
Giuseppe Attanasio, Instituto de Telecomunicações
Shaily Bhatt, Carnegie Mellon University
Siva Uday Sampreeth Chebolu, University of Houston
Wei-Fan Chen, Rheinische Friedrich-Wilhelms Universität Bonn
Jaemin Cho, University of North Carolina, Chapel Hill
Elizabeth Clark, Google
Amanda Cercas Curry, Bocconi University
Athiya Deviyani, School of Computer Science, Carnegie Mellon University
Sayan Ghosh, University of Southern California
Salvatore Giorgi, University of Pennsylvania
Karina H Halevy, Carnegie Mellon University
Shreya Havaldar, University of Pennsylvania
Chia-Chien Hung, NEC Laboratories Europe and Universität Mannheim
Akbar Karimi, Rheinische Friedrich-Wilhelms Universität Bonn
Harmanpreet Kaur, University of Minnesota - Twin Cities
Vivek Kulkarni, University of California Santa Barbara
Jonathan K. Kummerfeld, University of Sydney
Hwanhee Lee, Chung-Ang University
Inna Wanyin Lin, University of Washington
Shijia Liu, Northeastern University
Li Lucy, Allen Institute for Artificial Intelligence and University of California Berkeley
Meryem M'hamdi, University of Southern California
Nicole Meister, Stanford University
Jimin Mun, Carnegie Mellon University
Monica Munnangi, Northeastern University
Matthias Orlikowski, Universität Bielefeld
Barbara Plank, Ludwig-Maximilians-Universität München and IT University of Copenhagen
Joan Plepi, Rheinische Friedrich-Wilhelms Universität Bonn
Jielin Qiu, Carnegie Mellon University
Hannah Rashkin, Google
Naba Rizvi, University of California, San Diego
Paul Röttger, Bocconi University
Vahid Sadiri Javadi, Technische Universität Chemnitz
Ian Stewart, Pacific Northwest National Laboratory
Zeerak Talat, Mohamed bin Zayed University of Artificial Intelligence
Anvesh Rao Vijjini, University of North Carolina, Chapel Hill
Akhila Yerukola, Carnegie Mellon University

Hye Sun Yun, Northeastern University

Volunteer

Mounika Marreddy, University of Bonn

Table of Contents

Program

Thursday, August 15, 2024

09:00 - 09:10 *Opening Remarks*

09:10 - 09:55 *Keynote 1*

09:55 - 10:30 *Oral Presentation 1*

10:30 - 11:00 *Coffee Break*

11:00 - 11:45 *Keynote 2*

11:45 - 13:45 *Poster Presentation*

Human Speech Perception in Noise: Can Large Language Models Paraphrase to Improve It?
Anupama Chingacham, Miaoran Zhang, Vera Demberg and Dietrich Klakow

Human-Centered Design Recommendations for LLM-as-a-judge
Qian Pan, Zahra Ashktorab, Michael Desmond, Martín Santillán Cooper, James M. Johnson, Rahul Nair, Elizabeth M. Daly and Werner Geyer

Parameter-Efficient Detoxification with Contrastive Decoding
Tong Niu, Caiming Xiong, Yingbo Zhou and Semih Yavuz

To What Extent Are Large Language Models Capable of Generating Substantial Reflections for Motivational Interviewing Counseling Chatbots? A Human Evaluation
Erkan Basar, Iris Hendrickx, Emiel Krahmer, Gert-Jan de Bruijn and Tibor Bosse

Vision-Language Models under Cultural and Inclusive Considerations
Antonia Karamolegkou, Phillip Rust, Ruixiang Cui, Yong Cao, Anders Søgaard and Daniel Hershcovich

Evaluating Large Language Models on Social Signal Sensitivity: An Appraisal Theory Approach
Zhen Wu, Ritam Dutt and Carolyn Rose

Aligning to Adults Is Easy, Aligning to Children Is Hard: A Study of Linguistic Alignment in Dialogue Systems
Dorothea French, Sidney D'Mello and Katharina Von Der Wense

[Non-Archival] Exploring Human-AI Interaction: A Case Study on the Diplomacy Game
Shumin Deng, Jintian Zhang, Ningyu Zhang and Bryan Hooi

[Non-Archival] Learning from Teaching Assistants to Formulate Subgoals for Programming Tasks: Exploring the Potential for AI Teaching Assistants
Changyoon Lee, Junho Myung, Jieun Han, Jiho Jin and Alice Oh

[Non-Archival] Reference-free Medical Multi-document Summary Evaluation Metric via Contrastive Learning
Jimin Lee and Hwanhee Lee

[Non-Archival] Offline RLHF Methods Need More Accurate Supervision Signals
Shiqi Wang, Zhengze Zhang, Wang Xiaoliang, Rui Zhao, Fei Tan and Nguyen Cam-Tu

[Non-Archival (Published Papers)] Direct Preference Optimization with an Offset
Afra Amini, Tim Vieira and Ryan Cotterell

[Non-Archival (Published Papers)] DOSA: A Dataset of Social Artifacts from Different Indian Geographical Subcultures
Agrima Seth, Sanchit Ahuja, Kalika Bali and Sunayana Sitaram

[Non-Archival (Published Papers)] Book2Dial: Generating Teacher Student Interactions from Textbooks for Cost-Effective Development of Educational Chatbots
Junling Wang, Jakub Macina, Nico Daheim, Sankalan Pal Chowdhury and Mrinmaya Sachan

[Non-Archival (Published Papers)] Evaluating Large Language Model Biases in Persona-Steered Generation
Andy Liu, Mona Diab and Daniel Fried

[Non-Archival (Published Papers)] My Answer is C": First-Token Probabilities Do Not Match Text Answers in Instruction-Tuned Language Models
Xinpeng Wang, Bolei Ma, Chengzhi Hu, Leon Weber-Genzel, Paul Röttger, Frauke Kreuter, Dirk Hovy and Barbara Plank

12:45 - 13:45 *Lunch*

13:45 - 14:15 *Keynote 3*

14:15 - 15:00 *Oral Presentation 2*

Thursday, August 15, 2024 (continued)

15:00 - 15:30	*Brainstorming Session*
15:30 - 16:00	*Coffee Break*
16:00 - 16:30	*Keynote 4*
16:30 - 17:25	*Panel Discussion*
17:25 - 17:30	*Closing Remarks*

Human Speech Perception in Noise: Can Large Language Models Paraphrase to Improve It?

Anupama Chingacham[1] **Miaoran Zhang**[1] **Vera Demberg**[1,2] **Dietrich Klakow**[1]
[1]Saarland University, Saarland Informatic Campus, Germany
[2]Max Planck Institute for Informatics, Germany
achingacham@lsv.uni-saarland.de

Abstract

Large Language Models (LLMs) can generate text by transferring style attributes like formality resulting in formal or informal text. However, instructing LLMs to generate text that when spoken, is more intelligible in an acoustically difficult environment, is an underexplored topic. We conduct the first study to *evaluate LLMs on a novel task of generating acoustically intelligible paraphrases* for better human speech perception in noise. Our experiments in English demonstrated that with standard prompting, LLMs struggle to control the non-textual attribute, *i.e.,* acoustic intelligibility, while efficiently capturing the desired textual attributes like semantic equivalence. To remedy this issue, we propose a simple prompting approach, *prompt-and-select*, which generates paraphrases by decoupling the desired textual and non-textual attributes in the text generation pipeline. Our approach resulted in a 40% relative improvement in human speech perception, by paraphrasing utterances that are highly distorted in a listening condition with babble noise at signal-to-noise ratio (SNR) -5 dB. This study reveals the limitation of LLMs in capturing non-textual attributes, and our proposed method showcases the potential of using LLMs for better human speech perception in noise.[1]

1 Introduction

Paraphrase generation is the task of rephrasing a sentence while retaining its meaning (Bhagat and Hovy, 2013). Humans perform paraphrasing in spoken conversations, to enable their listeners to perceive spoken messages as intended (Bulyko et al., 2005; Bohus and Rudnicky, 2008). Motivated by human speech production strategies, paraphrasing has also been applied to speech synthesis systems, to enhance the quality, naturalness (Nakatsu and White, 2006; Boidin et al., 2009), and intelligibility of synthetic speech, especially in challenging acoustic conditions (Zhang et al., 2013). Recent explorations on why certain sentences are more intelligible than their paraphrases showed that, the observed intelligibility gain in a noisy listening environment is attributed to the rephrasing, which introduces more acoustic cues that survived the masking effect of the noise (Chingacham et al., 2021, 2023). In other words, the enhanced speech perception with paraphrasing is driven by noise-robust acoustic cues.

The potential of paraphrasing is however, seldom used to build human-like spoken dialogue systems that are adaptive to human listeners' perception errors in noise, presumably due to the limited investigations to generate paraphrases that are acoustically more intelligible in a noise condition. Prior studies relied on human annotations to identify the ideal paraphrase among a set of candidates (Nakatsu and White, 2006; Zhang et al., 2013; Chingacham et al., 2023), with little discussion on generating intelligible paraphrases. This raises the question of *how to generate text that is semantically equivalent to and acoustically more intelligible than the given input sentence, for a noisy environment.* We refer to this task as **Paraphrase to Improve Speech Perception in Noise** (PI-SPiN).

This task is particularly interesting in the context of generative LLMs, which have shown incredible performance in natural language generation (NLG) tasks such as paraphrase generation and dialogue generation (Radford et al., 2019; Wei et al., 2022; Li et al., 2024). Moreover, recent studies have demonstrated LLMs' capability to control text generation for a wide range of style attributes like sentiment, syntax, formality, and politeness (Zhang et al., 2023; Sun et al., 2023a). PI-SPiN differs from those controllable text generation problems, as it aims to generate text that satisfies the desired textual attributes (e.g., semantic equivalence), in

[1]Our code and data are available at https://github.com/uds-lsv/llm_eval_PI-SPiN.

Proceedings of the 1st Human-Centered Large Language Modeling Workshop, pages 1–15
August 15, 2024 ©2024 Association for Computational Linguistics

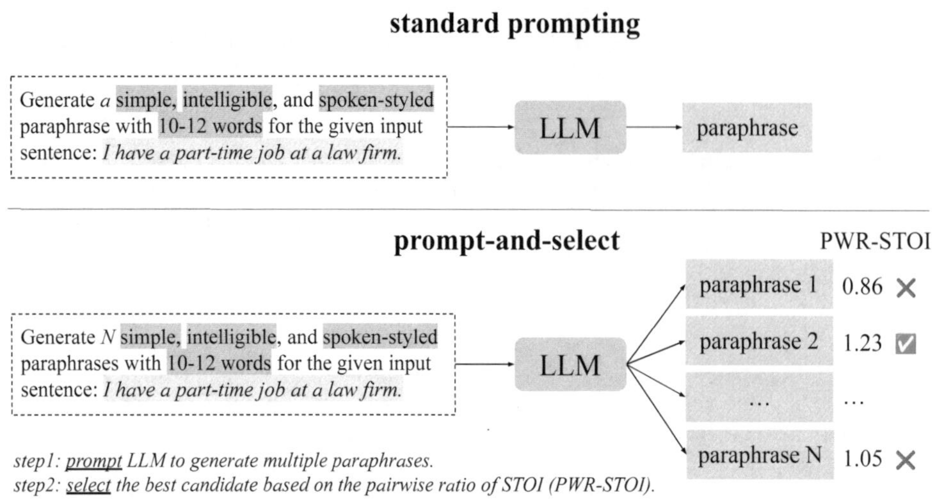

Figure 1: A schematic representation of the *prompt-and-select* and standard prompting approach to generate acoustically intelligible paraphrase in a noisy environment. A speech intelligibility metric, short-time objective intelligibility measure (STOI) is employed to select the paraphrase that is more likely to improve speech perception.

addition to the non-textual attribute (*i.e.* acoustic intelligibility), which is hard to describe textually.

To explore the potential of LLMs in PI-SPiN, we proposed to *evaluate LLMs' inherent capability to generate acoustically intelligible paraphrases*, without any model fine-tuning. Through standard prompting methods like zero-shot learning (ZSL), we found that the model was able to capture textual attributes, while consistently struggling to improve acoustic intelligibility. We also observed that increasing the description of the desired non-textual attribute in the prompt only confuses the model, and it may even lead to a deterioration in textual attributes that were achievable otherwise.

To effectively utilize LLMs for generating acoustically intelligible paraphrases, we propose a simple approach called *prompt-and-select*, which guides paraphrase generation by introducing the desired non-textual attribute in a post-processing step (see Figure 1). It is a two-step process beginning with prompting the LLM to generate multiple candidates and then selecting the best candidate based on acoustic intelligibility, which is hard to capture in textual mode alone. By conducting a human evaluation with native English listeners, who have no hearing impairments, we verified that the LLM-generated paraphrases via *prompt-and-select* approach are indeed more intelligible than original sentences, in a listening environment with babble noise at SNR -5 dB.[2]

[2]See definitions of babble noise and SNR in Appendix A.

Our main contributions are as follows:

- We conduct an elaborate study on the evaluation of LLMs on a novel task called PI-SPiN.
- Our results illustrate the weakness of standard textual prompting to control a non-textual attribute – acoustic intelligibility.
- Our proposed approach *prompt-and-select* is an effective solution to generate paraphrases that are more acoustically intelligible.

2 Related Work

Acoustic Intelligibility. Speech perception has been a long-standing research topic in speech science (Kalikow et al., 1977; Luce and Pisoni, 1998; McArdle and Wilson, 2008), which contributed towards a better understanding of human (*mis*)hearing. More specifically, several human perception experiments were conducted to investigate the intelligibility of speech tokens such as vowels (Pickett, 1957; Cutler et al., 2004), consonants (Weber and Smits, 2003; Jürgens and Brand, 2009), words in isolation (Luce and Pisoni, 1998; Clopper et al., 2010; Wilson and Cates, 2008), words in context (Kalikow et al., 1977; Uslar et al., 2011; Chingacham et al., 2021), especially in noisy environments. While several studies showcased the influence of linguistic characteristics such as predictability (Kalikow et al., 1977), syntactic complexity (Uslar et al., 2011; Carroll and Ruigendijk, 2013; van Knijff et al., 2018), and lexical features (Luce and

Pisoni, 1998; McArdle and Wilson, 2008), on the intelligibility of utterances in noise, there is limited explorations in utilizing the linguistic potential to improve acoustic intelligibility in noise.

We share the motivation to improve speech perception in noise using paraphrases with early studies (Cox and Vinagre, 2004; Nakatsu and White, 2006; Zhang et al., 2013; Chingacham et al., 2023). Nakatsu and White (2006) proposed to train a reranker to select the paraphrases that are more likely to sound natural, when synthesized. They generated multiple paraphrases for each sentence mainly by modifying the word order and replacing a few lexical units in the original sentence. On the other hand, Zhang et al. (2013) proposed an objective measure to distinguish the intelligibility difference among paraphrases that are of the same syntactic type, thereby restricting the type of sentential paraphrases. More recently, Chingacham et al. (2023) investigated the potential of improving intelligibility by considering a larger set of paraphrase types, which are generated using modern paraphrasing models. However, our work is distinct from theirs as we explore LLMs' inherent ability to generate acoustically intelligible paraphrases.

LLM Evaluation. Given the rapid growth of LLMs such as ChatGPT and GPT-4 (OpenAI, 2023), there has been a surge of research interest towards a holistic evaluation of their capabilities (Chang et al., 2024). Recent studies have attempted to examine their performance across diverse tasks, such as machine translation (Hendy et al., 2023; Zhu et al., 2023), text summarization (Yang et al., 2023; Pu and Demberg, 2023), etc; and also aspects of multilinguality (Lai et al., 2023b; Ahuja et al., 2023) and multimodality (Bang et al., 2023). Close to our work, there have been a few studies looking into the controllable generation ability of LLMs. Lai et al. (2023a) explore the potential of ChatGPT as a text-style transfer evaluator. Sun et al. (2023b) present a systematic study on ten controllable generation benchmarks. Notably, their control factors are derived from the language perspective (e.g., sentiment and number), whereas our work pioneers the investigation of the potential of LLMs as an acoustically intelligible paraphrase generator.

3 PI-SPiN Task Description

Typically, the paraphrase generation task focuses on generating text that is semantically equivalent to the given input text. However, the PI-SPiN task aims at generating text that is semantically equivalent to, as well as, acoustically more intelligible than the original input text, in an adverse listening condition.

For example, consider the following paraphrase triplet (s_1, s_2, s_3) from the Paraphrases-in-Noise (PiN) dataset[3] (Chingacham et al., 2023):

s_1: *"i was raised in a generation we did need all those things."*

s_2: *"we did need all those things when i was a child."*

s_3: *"we did need all those things when i was young."*

s_1 is a sentence retrieved from a spoken corpus, while s_2 and s_3 are outcomes of a paraphrase generation pipeline. Though all sentences are semantically equivalent to each other, they exhibited a significant difference in acoustic intelligibility under noise. More precisely, when these sentences were uttered in a difficult listening condition with babble noise at an SNR of -5 dB, humans perceived s_2 with fewer errors in perception compared to s_1, while s_3 was perceived much worse than s_1. The better intelligibility of utterances can be attributed to both linguistic features like predictability (Kalikow et al., 1977), syntactic structure (Uslar et al., 2013), as well as acoustic features like the underlying sounds of the utterance (Luce and Pisoni, 1998). In the more recent investigations on the intelligibility difference among paraphrases (Chingacham et al., 2023), it was shown that the better intelligibility of s_2 in such high noise environments is mainly driven by the noise-robust acoustic cues that are defined by both the constituting sounds as well as the noise signal. PI-SPiN aims to generate paraphrases (like s_2) that are likely to improve human speech perception in such noisy conditions.

Speech intelligibility in noise is better when sentences are simple (Carroll and Ruigendijk, 2013), shorter (Coene et al., 2016), and linguistically more predictive (Valentini-Botinhao and Wester, 2014). However, the intelligibility of an utterance in noise is not only driven by its underlying text. The perception is also influenced by the acoustic cues that survived the masking effect of the background noise (Cooke, 2006). Hence, PI-SPiN is a

[3]See Appendix B for more samples.

text generation task, that involves both textual attributes like semantic equivalence and a non-textual attribute that captures the noise-robustness of an utterance.

To generate the acoustic realization of a sentence, we used the Tacotron2 text-to-speech (TTS) system, which demonstrated performance on par with that of a professional voice talent (Shen et al., 2018). More specifically, we used the Tacotron2 model[4] pre-trained on the LJSpeech dataset by SpeechBrain (Ravanelli et al., 2021). Further, to create the noise-distorted signals, the clean audio signals underwent a noise-mixing procedure using an open-sourced tool, *audio-SNR*.[5] The babble noise from the NOISEX-92 dataset (Varga and Steeneken, 1993) was mixed with clean audio at SNR-5 dB. To determine whether the generated text satisfies the desired outcome, we primarily relied on automatic metrics, which are discussed in detail in the following section.

4 Experimental Setup

Model. For all our experiments, we used *ChatGPT*[6] (Ouyang et al., 2022), which is one of the most popular LLMs. It has shown impressive performance on paraphrase generation with textual style attributes, while its ability on acoustically intelligible paraphrasing remains unclear. We adopt default parameters (temperature=1.0, top_p=1.0) for the API calls.

Dataset. The evaluation dataset consists of 300 short sentences, which are spoken in a conversational scenario. The dataset is created by filtering out sentences with 10 to 12 words from the top 1000 lines of the speech corpus, Switchboard (Godfrey et al., 1992).

Metrics. Human evaluation is the gold standard for most text-generation tasks. However, human evaluation is expensive and time-consuming, which limits the scale of evaluation. Thus, we perform an automatic evaluation of the whole evaluation dataset and a human evaluation of a subset of the dataset. For automatic evaluation, we employed a range of metrics, which determine the semantic equivalence between the input and output texts, as well as, the linguistic and acoustic features that contribute to the acoustic intelligibility in noise.

[4]https://huggingface.co/speechbrain/tts-tacotron2-ljspeech

[5]https://github.com/Sato-Kunihiko/audio-SNR

[6]Version: gpt-3.5-turbo

1. Semantic equivalence. Semantic Textual Similarity (STS) measures how similar two texts are in terms of their meaning. In the past, several STS scores were proposed (Bär et al., 2012; Han et al., 2013). More recently, Zhang et al. (2020) proposed BERTScore, which has shown encouraging results in correctly identifying the semantic equivalence/distance between two texts. For all our evaluations, the STS score is the BERTScore-f1 calculated using the distilled BERT model (Sanh et al., 2019). The higher the STS value, the better the semantic equivalence between two texts.

2. Lexical deviation. Lexical deviation (LD) shows to what extent two texts are similar or different in terms of their surface form. The difference in wording between the two texts is particularly interesting for paraphrase generation. Bandel et al. (2022) showed that the deviation in the linguistic forms of paraphrases is one of the critical factors that decides its quality – high-quality paraphrases exhibit high LD, as well as, high STS as they differ lexically, yet maintain the semantics. As defined in Liu and Soh (2022), we used the overlap in lexical tokens of the uncased lemmatized form of two texts to capture the lexical deviation between the input sentence and the model-generated paraphrase. The higher the LD score, the more difference in paraphrased wording.

3. Utterance length. It is a textual attribute that influences acoustic intelligibility, as it was observed that shorter sentences introduce fewer misperceptions in noise (Chingacham et al., 2023). Though paraphrases of shorter lengths are more likely to be perceived correctly, shorter paraphrases may risk missing some semantics of the original text. Hence, it is critical to evaluate utterance length along with semantic equivalence. To measure utterance length in terms of phonemes (*i.e.* PhLen), we used a grapheme-to-phoneme model[7] to generate the phonemic transcript of a sentence. Further, to compare the length within each input-output pair, the *pairwise ratio of PhLen* is calculated by dividing the length of the model output by that of its input sentence (denoted as *PWR*-PhLen). Thus, when the model-generated text is similar to the input text, *PWR*-PhLen value is close to 1.0, while a value much less than 1.0 reflects that the model-generated text is considerably shorter than the original text.

[7]https://pypi.org/project/g2p-en/

Prompt-ID	Prompt
$p_{zsl-low}$	Generate an **intelligible paraphrase** for the following input sentence: `{input text}`
$p_{zsl-med}$	Generate a **simple**, **intelligible**, and **spoken-styled paraphrase** with **10-12 words** for the following input sentence: `{input text}`
$p_{zsl-high}$	**For a noisy listening environment with babble noise at SNR -5**, generate a **simple**, **intelligible**, and **spoken-styled paraphrase** with **10-12 words**, for the following input sentence: `{input text}`

Table 1: Three prompts used in standard prompting, with an increasing level of detail in the task objective. Bold-faced words are task-specific keywords in the prompt statement.

4. Linguistic predictability. Several studies in the past have shown that when lexical tokens are more predictable from the context, word misperceptions are less likely to occur (Kalikow et al., 1977; Uslar et al., 2013; Valentini-Botinhao and Wester, 2014; Schoof and Rosen, 2015; Bhandari et al., 2021). Thus, we considered the perplexity (PPL) score determined by a pre-trained language model, GPT-2[8] (Radford et al., 2019) to estimate the linguistic predictability of a sentence. To compare the linguistic predictability among input and output texts, the *pairwise ratio of the perplexity* is calculated by dividing the PPL of model-generated text by the input sentence PPL (denoted as *PWR*-PPL). Higher PPL scores indicate lesser linguistic predictability. Thus, a *PWR*-PPL value less than 1.0 indicates that the model-generated text is more predictable than the input text.

5. Acoustic Intelligibility. The acoustic intelligibility of an utterance in a noisy environment is primarily driven by the acoustic cues that survived the energetic masking of the noise – utterances with better noise-robust acoustic cues are better perceived in noise (Cooke, 2006; Tang and Cooke, 2016). We use the Speech Intelligibility (SI) metric, STOI (Taal et al., 2010), to capture the acoustic intelligibility of an utterance. STOI is a non-textual attribute, as it measures the mean correlation of short-time envelopes between the clean and noisy audio signals of an utterance. The higher the STOI score, the higher the noise-robustness of an utterance. Similar to other pairwise ratios, the *pairwise ratio of STOI* (*PWR*-STOI) is calculated by dividing the STOI of model-generated text by the input text STOI. Thus, PI-SPiN aims at generating paraphrases with *PWR*-STOI values above 1.0 indicating that the model output is acoustically more intelligible than the input sentences.

All pairwise ratios range between 0.0 and $+\infty$, while STS and LD range between 0.0 and 1.0. For the evaluation, we report each of these metrics, averaging across the evaluation dataset.

5 Evaluating LLMs for PI-SPiN

In our experiments, an LLM is prompted to generate a paraphrase for each input sentence in the evaluation set with a prompt template: `{prompt prefix} + {input text}`. In the following section, we described two prompting methods that we employed and evaluated for the task.

5.1 Standard Prompting

In this setting, the model is prompted to generate an intelligible paraphrase given an input sentence in a zero-shot manner. As shown in Table 1, we investigate three types of prompts, which describe the desired attributes with different granularity: low ($p_{zsl-low}$), medium ($p_{zsl-med}$), and high ($p_{zsl-high}$). With the increasing number of task-specific tokens in the prompt, the task description is more detailed. Prompts are designed by including keywords like '*paraphrase*' and '*intelligible*' that represent the desired outcome. Additionally, a few more tokens like '*10-12 words*' and '*spoken-styled*' were used in the prompt to ensure that the generated paraphrase adheres to the length and style of input sentences. We hypothesize that with additional task-oriented tokens in the prompt, the model will steer the paraphrase generation by optimizing the intelligibility.

Results and Analysis Table 2 summarizes the results of all three prompts that we used in standard prompting. We observed that ChatGPT can generate high-quality paraphrases as indicated by high scores for semantic equivalence and lexical

[8]Version: `distilgpt2`

Prompt-ID	STS↑	LD↑	*PWR*-PhLen↓	*PWR*-PPL↓	*PWR*-STOI ↑
$p_{zsl-low}$	0.852	0.699	1.343*	1.086	0.992
$p_{zsl-med}$	0.860	0.668	1.119*	1.042	0.991
$p_{zsl-high}$	0.837	0.729	1.250*	1.236*	1.005

Table 2: An automatic evaluation of paraphrases generated by different prompts. Pairwise ratios (*PWR*) significantly different from 1.0 ($p < 0.05$) are marked with an asterisk (*). They indicate the significant difference between the model-generated output and the input text.[9]

Prompt-ID		Sentences
—	`{input text}`	*I also have a part-time job at a law firm.*
$p_{zsl-low}$	`{output}`	*Additionally, I am employed part-time at a law firm.*
$p_{zsl-med}$	`{output}`	*I work part time at a law firm as well.*
$p_{zsl-high}$	`{output}`	***In a busy environment with loud chatter**, I work part-time at a law office.*
—	`{input text}`	*Is your father's cafe, one that you could cater out of?*
$p_{zsl-low}$	`{output}`	*Can you use your father's cafe as a location for catering purposes?*
$p_{zsl-med}$	`{output}`	*Could you use your father's cafe as a catering venue?*
$p_{zsl-high}$	`{output}`	*Can your dad's café be used for catering **in a noisy setting**?*
—	`{input text}`	*I believe that the cure for polio is already founded.*
$p_{zsl-low}$	`{output}`	*I hold the belief that the remedy for polio has already been discovered.*
$p_{zsl-med}$	`{output}`	*I think the polio cure has already been discovered.*
$p_{zsl-high}$	`{output}`	*I think polio's cure has already been discovered **in a noisy setting.***
—	`{input text}`	*I think you can do that for a little while.*
$p_{zsl-low}$	`{output}`	*I believe you have the capability to do that temporarily.*
$p_{zsl-med}$	`{output}`	*I believe you can manage that temporarily.*
$p_{zsl-high}$	`{output}`	*I believe you can manage it temporarily **amidst the loud chatter.***

Table 3: A qualitative analysis of model-generated text, `{output}`, for a given `{input text}` under three standard prompts: $p_{zsl-low}, p_{zsl-med}, p_{zsl-high}$. The prompt $p_{zsl-high}$ generates several tokens that are irrelevant (bold-faced words) to the task objective.

deviation (*i.e.* STS and LD). More importantly, we found that the length of paraphrases generated by the prompt $p_{zsl-med}$ (PhLen = 42.08) is considerably shorter than those generated with the prompt $p_{zsl-low}$ (PhLen = 50.67), indicating the effectiveness of additional keywords in $p_{zsl-med}$ to control a textual attribute – length. However, the non-textual attribute, acoustic intelligibility (*i.e.* STOI) of model-generated paraphrases is not significantly different from their corresponding input sentences as reflected by the *PWR*-STOI scores being not significantly different from 1.0. Furthermore, paraphrases generated with a detailed task description in $p_{zsl-high}$, also resulted in a similar observation – **LLM struggles to improve the non-textual attribute while controlling textual attributes appropriately**.

[9]See Appendix C for the absolute scores of different metrics.

Compared to $p_{zsl-low}$ and $p_{zsl-med}$, $p_{zsl-high}$ resulted in worse performance, indicated by considerably longer output texts despite prompting to control length (*PWR*-PhLen = 1.250) and output texts that are linguistically less predictive (*PWR*-PPL = 1.236). It is also reflected in a higher lexical deviation (LD = 0.723) at the expense of lower textual similarity between input and output (STS = 0.837). To have a deep understanding of its behavior, we conducted a qualitative analysis as shown in Table 3. We noticed that the **additional context of the non-textual attribute confused the model in understanding the task objective and resulted in model hallucination**. In sum, using standard prompting may not effectively elicit the model's ability to generate paraphrases with the intended non-textual attribute, which is beyond the model's comprehension.[10]

[10]In Appendix D, we also conducted a preliminary study

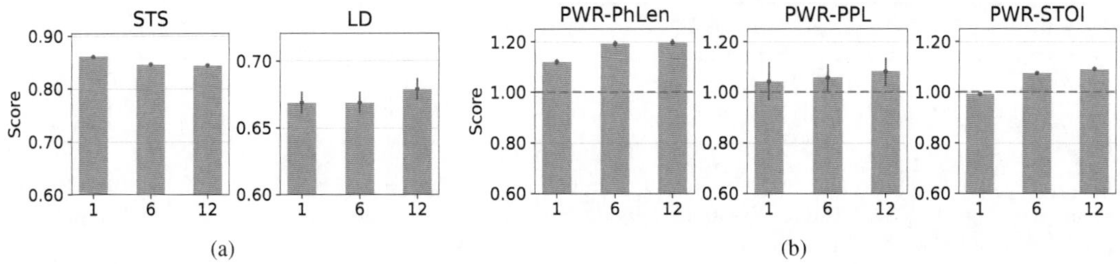

Figure 2: An automatic evaluation of the standard prompting ($n = 1$) and the proposed prompt-and-select ($n > 1$) approach. The *X*-axis is the number of candidates generated (n) and the *Y*-axis is the mean scores (with error bars at 95% confidence interval). The reference line in Fig. (b) marks when the input text feature is the same as the output text feature. Increasing n improves the pairwise ratio of acoustic intelligibility (*PWR*-STOI), but it comes with a trade-off on semantic equivalence (STS).[11]

5.2 PAS: Prompt-and-Select

Prior studies on dialogue generation (Boidin et al., 2009; Nakatsu and White, 2006; Weston et al., 2018) have demonstrated the utility of a simple yet effective pipeline of controlling text generation in two steps: first generating a candidate set of dialogues, and then selecting the best candidate based on the task requirement. Similarly, we proposed to decompose the current task into a two-step process: (1) **prompt** the LLM to generate multiple output texts that are semantically equivalent to the input text and (2) **select** the best candidate based on the acoustic intelligibility.

Our approach is similar to the *prompt-and-rerank* method proposed in (Suzgun et al., 2022). However, our approach deviates from theirs mainly in two ways: (1) instead of using beam search at the decoding phase, we propose to utilize the potential of an LLM to generate multiple (n) candidates that exhibit the desired textual attributes and (2) the best candidate selection is based on a metric (*i.e. PWR*-STOI) that represents a non-textual attribute, which is not considered in prior studies.

For the first step of paraphrase generation, we perform zero-shot prompting with an appropriate task description, $p_{zsl-med}$. Thus, $p_{zsl-med}$ is the prompt that generates exactly one candidate and involves no selection; it is also referred to as $p_{pas(n=1)}$. However, to generate multiple paraphrases (eg: $n = 6$), the prompt statement can be simply modified to include the n value, as shown below

- *Generate **6** simple, intelligible, and spoken-styled paraphrases with 10-12 words for the given input sentence: {*`input text`*}*

Following the creation of the candidate set, STOI scores are calculated for all model-generated text as well as the input text, by first synthesizing the clean utterances and then mixing babble noise at SNR -5 dB. Finally, the candidate with the highest *PWR*-STOI is selected as the model output.

Results and Analysis We begin our analysis by comparing the results of standard prompting ($n = 1$) with the PAS approach, involving 6 candidates ($n = 6$). As shown in Figure 2a, PAS showcased a high quality of paraphrase generation as indicated by high STS and high LD, similar to the standard prompting setup. Similarly, Figure 2b illustrates that other textual attributes like linguistic predictability (*PWR*-PPL = 1.056) and utterance length (*PWR*-PhLen = 1.192) of the PAS approach resulted in similar outcomes of the standard prompting method – output texts are a bit longer than input texts, while their linguistic predictability scores are similar. Importantly, compared to the standard prompting, the prompt-and-select approach yielded a noticeably high *PWR*-STOI ($\mu = 1.074$, $p < 0.05$), which is significantly above 1.0. This indicates that the model-generated text is considerably more intelligible than their corresponding input sentences in the given noise condition. We can see more clearly from Figure 2b that PAS ($n = 6$) leads to a relative improvement of 8.4% in *PWR*-STOI compared to the standard prompting ($n = 1$). Our findings suggest that **introducing the desired non-textual attribute in a post-processing step is a potential framework to generate desired text with multi-modal behavior**.

This raises a follow-up question of whether generating more candidates in the first step further improves the overall *PWR*-STOI of generated para-

on in-context learning, suggesting that demonstrations are not helpful in capturing the non-textual attribute.

[11]See Appendix C for the absolute scores of different metrics with varying numbers of candidates.

Subset	STS↑	LD↑	*PWR*-PhLen ↓	*PWR*-PPL ↓	*PWR*-STOI ↑	*PWR*-Sent-Int ↑
top_{30}	0.831	0.737	1.189*	1.428	1.22*	**1.70***
$random_{30}$	0.848	0.683	1.157*	1.314	1.07*	1.06

Table 4: The automatic and human evaluation of text generated with $p_{pas(n=6)}$. Evaluation on two subsets: top 30 pairs with highest *PWR*-STOI (top_{30}) and randomly selected 30 pairs ($random_{30}$). *PWR*-Sent-Int captures the pairwise ratio of human speech perception in noise. * marks values significantly above 1.0 ($p < 0.05$).

phrases. To this end, we modify the number of candidates (n) in the prompt statement to double the candidate pool size. We found that by increasing the candidate set, there is an improvement in acoustic intelligibility. However, when n is increased from 6 to 12, there was only a limited improvement of 1.6% in *PWR*-STOI. On the other hand, we observed that textual attributes like linguistic predictability and lexical deviation are not significantly different under varying n values.

Interestingly, the pair-wise ratio of sentence length slightly increased, with more choices in the candidate selection; however, the overall *PWR*-PhLen in this approach is still below the standard prompting setup with no tokens to control length ($p_{zsl-low}$). Increasing n from 6 to 12 slightly reduced the overall semantic equivalence between the model input and output paraphrase. This indicates that the choice of n introduces a trade-off between the improvement in acoustic intelligibility (*PWR*-STOI) and the overall semantic equivalence (STS) and one has to choose n considering this trade-off between the gain in non-textual attribute and the need for semantic equivalence.

5.3 Human Evaluation

In addition to the evaluation with automatic metrics, we also conducted a human evaluation to verify whether the model output in the PAS setup (using $p_{pas(n=6)}$) is indeed more intelligible than their corresponding input sentences. For the human perception experiment, we created two subsets of the evaluation dataset of 300 pairs: $random_{30}$ and top_{30}. $random_{30}$ is a set of 30 pairs randomly selected from the evaluation dataset, while top_{30} is the top 30 input-output pairs that exhibited the larger improvements in STOI scores.

We followed the experiment design of Chingacham et al. (2023) to capture the human speech perception of an utterance in a (noisy) listening setup. After synthesizing the noisy utterances of each sentence using a TTS (Shen et al., 2018) and a noise-mixing tool (audio-SNR), participants were asked to listen and transcribe each sentence. Every utterance in the dataset was listened to by six different participants. For each listening instance, the edit distance between the phonemic transcriptions of the actual and transcribed text is measured to determine the rate of correct recognition. Furthermore, the sentence-level intelligibility (Sent-Int) of each utterance is calculated by averaging the correct recognition rates exhibited by the six listeners.

The perception experiment was conducted with 24 native English listeners with no hearing impairments (14 females and 10 males; average age = 30.71). After data collection, we calculated the pairwise ratio of sentence-level intelligibility (*PWR*-Sent-Int) by dividing the Sent-Int scores of the output paraphrase by their corresponding input sentence. A mean score of *PWR*-Sent-Int significantly above 1.0 indicates that the model-generated paraphrase is significantly more intelligible than the input sentence, in a given listening condition.

Results and Analysis As illustrated in Table 4, top_{30} items signify that the model-output paraphrases have considerably improved the human perception in a noisy listening condition. We observed that the overall human speech perception of model-output paraphrases (Sent-Int = 0.66) was considerably higher than the input sentences (Sent-Int = 0.47), introducing a 40% **relative gain in the overall intelligibility**. This is also reflected in the *PWR*-Sent-Int score that is significantly above 1.0.

We observed the *PWR*-Sent-Int of $random_{30}$ is not significantly above 1.0, even though the *PWR*-STOI is significantly above 1.0. With further analysis of two subsets, we found that the mean STOI of input sentences in top_{30} ($\mu = 0.507$) is significantly less than $random_{30}$ ($\mu = 0.561$). This means that $random_{30}$ consists of sentences that are better intelligible in noise. Also, we observed a strong negative correlation ($r = -0.442, p < 0.001$) between the STOI of input sentences and the gain in intelligibility (*PWR*-Sent-Int), which highlighted the limited benefits of paraphrasing input sentences in $random_{30}$. However, top_{30} consists of all input sentences, which are more likely to benefit from paraphrasing in noisy listening conditions and they reflected the same in the human evaluation. We conclude with the observation PAS is a simple yet effective solution to alleviate the struggles of LLM to generate text with textual and non-textual attributes, without model fine-tuning.

6 Conclusion

In this work, we evaluate LLMs on acoustically intelligible paraphrase generation for better human speech perception in noise. Our results demonstrate the limitations of LLMs in controlling text generation with a non-textual attribute – acoustic intelligibility. To alleviate the struggles of LLMs in generating text that satisfies both textual and non-textual attributes, we proposed a simple yet effective approach called *prompt-and-select*. With human evaluation, we found that when the original utterances are highly prone to misperceptions in noise, prompt-and-select can introduce 40% of relative improvement in human perception. We hope the findings of this work inspire further explorations to control LLMs' text generation with different real-world context cues, thereby building more human-like agents. For future work, we could consider two approaches to improve LLMs on this task: 1) fine-tuning LLMs with a large parallel dataset consisting of sentences and their corresponding intelligible paraphrases, and 2) incorporating the acoustic representation of the utterances to control the paraphrase generation.

Limitations

The proposed "prompt-and-select" approach relies on the efficacy of STOI scores to identify the best candidate which is more likely to be perceived correctly in noise. In other words, this approach requires a metric that accurately estimates the desired non-textual attribute. This could be a limitation for problems that require human annotations for candidate selection. Additionally, the current approach introduces an overhead in computation and inference time, due to multiple generations and STOI calculation that involves speech synthesis and noise-mixing procedure. Further investigations are required to study the trade-off between the benefits of paraphrasing and the cost of additional resources. Moreover, our study only evaluated ChatGPT, one of the representative LLMs, due to budget and resource constraints. We believe that a holistic evaluation covering more open-source models, such as Mistral (Jiang et al., 2023) and Llama 3 (Meta, 2024), will be beneficial to deepen our understanding of LLM capabilities.

Ethics statement

In this work, generative LLMs are evaluated for a new task without model fine-tuning. It is an impactful step to democratize LLMs for research facilities with limited data and computing resources. We conducted a human evaluation on Prolific, ensuring that all participants were paid (9 GBP) for their service, considering the recommended minimum wage per hour in the UK, in 2023. Also, we ensured to provide an inclusive environment for our participants in the perception experiment, providing non-binary options to mark their gender identity.

Acknowledgements

We would like to thank anonymous reviewers for their valuable feedback. This work was funded by the Deutsche Forschungsgemeinschaft (DFG, German Research Foundation) – project-id 232722074 – SFB 1102.

References

Kabir Ahuja, Harshita Diddee, Rishav Hada, Millicent Ochieng, Krithika Ramesh, Prachi Jain, Akshay Nambi, Tanuja Ganu, Sameer Segal, Mohamed Ahmed, Kalika Bali, and Sunayana Sitaram. 2023. MEGA: Multilingual evaluation of generative AI. In *Proceedings of the 2023 Conference on Empirical Methods in Natural Language Processing*, pages 4232–4267, Singapore. Association for Computational Linguistics.

Elron Bandel, Ranit Aharonov, Michal Shmueli-Scheuer, Ilya Shnayderman, Noam Slonim, and Liat Ein Dor. 2022. Quality controlled paraphrase generation. In *Proceedings of the 60th Annual Meeting of the Association for Computational Linguistics (Volume 1: Long Papers)*, pages 596–609.

Yejin Bang, Samuel Cahyawijaya, Nayeon Lee, Wenliang Dai, Dan Su, Bryan Wilie, Holy Lovenia, Ziwei Ji, Tiezheng Yu, Willy Chung, Quyet V. Do, Yan Xu, and Pascale Fung. 2023. A multitask, multilingual, multimodal evaluation of ChatGPT on reasoning, hallucination, and interactivity. In *Proceedings of the 13th International Joint Conference on Natural Language Processing and the 3rd Conference of the Asia-Pacific Chapter of the Association for Computational Linguistics (Volume 1: Long Papers)*, pages 675–718,

Nusa Dua, Bali. Association for Computational Linguistics.

Daniel Bär, Chris Biemann, Iryna Gurevych, and Torsten Zesch. 2012. UKP: Computing semantic textual similarity by combining multiple content similarity measures. In **SEM 2012: The First Joint Conference on Lexical and Computational Semantics – Volume 1: Proceedings of the main conference and the shared task, and Volume 2: Proceedings of the Sixth International Workshop on Semantic Evaluation (SemEval 2012)*, pages 435–440, Montréal, Canada. Association for Computational Linguistics.

Rahul Bhagat and Eduard Hovy. 2013. What is a paraphrase? *Computational Linguistics*, 39(3):463–472.

Pratik Bhandari, Vera Demberg, and Jutta Kray. 2021. Semantic predictability facilitates comprehension of degraded speech in a graded manner. *Frontiers in Psychology*, 12.

Dan Bohus and Alexander I Rudnicky. 2008. Sorry, i didn't catch that! an investigation of non-understanding errors and recovery strategies. *Recent trends in discourse and dialogue*, pages 123–154.

Cedric Boidin, Verena Rieser, Lonneke van der Plas, Oliver Lemon, and Jonathan Chevelu. 2009. Predicting how it sounds: Re-ranking dialogue prompts based on tts quality for adaptive spoken dialogue systems. In *Tenth Annual Conference of the International Speech Communication Association*.

Tom Brown, Benjamin Mann, Nick Ryder, Melanie Subbiah, Jared D Kaplan, Prafulla Dhariwal, Arvind Neelakantan, Pranav Shyam, Girish Sastry, Amanda Askell, Sandhini Agarwal, Ariel Herbert-Voss, Gretchen Krueger, Tom Henighan, Rewon Child, Aditya Ramesh, Daniel Ziegler, Jeffrey Wu, Clemens Winter, Chris Hesse, Mark Chen, Eric Sigler, Mateusz Litwin, Scott Gray, Benjamin Chess, Jack Clark, Christopher Berner, Sam McCandlish, Alec Radford, Ilya Sutskever, and Dario Amodei. 2020. Language models are few-shot learners. In *Advances in Neural Information Processing Systems*, volume 33, pages 1877–1901. Curran Associates, Inc.

Ivan Bulyko, Katrin Kirchhoff, Mari Ostendorf, and Julie Goldberg. 2005. Error-correction detection and response generation in a spoken dialogue system. *Speech Communication*, 45(3):271–288.

Rebecca Carroll and Esther Ruigendijk. 2013. The effects of syntactic complexity on processing sentences in noise. *Journal of psycholinguistic research*, 42(2):139–159.

Yupeng Chang, Xu Wang, Jindong Wang, Yuan Wu, Linyi Yang, Kaijie Zhu, Hao Chen, Xiaoyuan Yi, Cunxiang Wang, Yidong Wang, et al. 2024. A survey on evaluation of large language models. *ACM Transactions on Intelligent Systems and Technology*, 15(3):1–45.

Anupama Chingacham, Vera Demberg, and Dietrich Klakow. 2021. Exploring the Potential of Lexical Paraphrases for Mitigating Noise-Induced Comprehension Errors. In *Proc. Interspeech*, pages 1713–1717.

Anupama Chingacham, Vera Demberg, and Dietrich Klakow. 2023. A data-driven investigation of noise-adaptive utterance generation with linguistic modification. In *2022 IEEE Spoken Language Technology Workshop (SLT)*, pages 353–360. IEEE.

Cynthia G. Clopper, Janet B. Pierrehumbert, and Terrin N. Tamati. 2010. Lexical neighborhoods and phonological confusability in cross-dialect word recognition in noise. *Laboratory Phonology*, 1(1):65 – 92.

Martine Coene, Stefanie Krijger, Matthias Meeuws, Geert De Ceulaer, and Paul J Govaerts. 2016. Linguistic factors influencing speech audiometric assessment. *BioMed research international*, 2016.

Martin Cooke. 2006. A glimpsing model of speech perception in noise. *The JASA*, 119(3):1562–1573.

Stephen Cox and Lluis Vinagre. 2004. Modelling of confusions in aircraft call-signs. *Speech communication*, 42(3-4):289–312.

Anne Cutler, Andrea Weber, Roel Smits, and Nicole Cooper. 2004. Patterns of english phoneme confusions by native and non-native listeners. *The JASA*, 116(6):3668–3678.

Mangesh S Deshpande and Raghunath S Holambe. 2009. Speaker identification based on robust am-fm features. In *2009 Second International Conference on Emerging Trends in Engineering & Technology*, pages 880–884. IEEE.

John J. Godfrey, Edward C. Holliman, and Jane McDaniel. 1992. Switchboard: Telephone speech corpus for research and development. In *Proceedings of the 1992 IEEE ICASSP - Volume 1*, ICASSP'92, page 517–520. IEEE Computer Society.

Lushan Han, Abhay L Kashyap, Tim Finin, James Mayfield, and Jonathan Weese. 2013. Umbc_ebiquity-core: Semantic textual similarity systems. In *Second joint conference on lexical and computational semantics (* SEM), volume 1: Proceedings of the main conference and the shared task: Semantic textual similarity*, pages 44–52.

Amr Hendy, Mohamed Abdelrehim, Amr Sharaf, Vikas Raunak, Mohamed Gabr, Hitokazu Matsushita, Young Jin Kim, Mohamed Afify, and Hany Hassan Awadalla. 2023. How good are gpt models at machine translation? a comprehensive evaluation. *arXiv preprint arXiv:2302.09210*.

Albert Q. Jiang, Alexandre Sablayrolles, Arthur Mensch, Chris Bamford, Devendra Singh Chaplot, Diego de las Casas, Florian Bressand, Gianna Lengyel, Guillaume Lample, Lucile Saulnier, Lélio Renard Lavaud,

Marie-Anne Lachaux, Pierre Stock, Teven Le Scao, Thibaut Lavril, Thomas Wang, Timothée Lacroix, and William El Sayed. 2023. Mistral 7b. *Preprint*, arXiv:2310.06825.

Tim Jürgens and Thomas Brand. 2009. Microscopic prediction of speech recognition for listeners with normal hearing in noise using an auditory model. *The JASA*, 126(5):2635–2648.

Daniel N Kalikow, Kenneth N Stevens, and Lois L Elliott. 1977. Development of a test of speech intelligibility in noise using sentence materials with controlled word predictability. *The JASA*, 61(5):1337–1351.

Huiyuan Lai, Antonio Toral, and Malvina Nissim. 2023a. Multidimensional evaluation for text style transfer using chatgpt. *arXiv preprint arXiv:2304.13462*.

Viet Lai, Nghia Ngo, Amir Pouran Ben Veyseh, Hieu Man, Franck Dernoncourt, Trung Bui, and Thien Nguyen. 2023b. ChatGPT beyond English: Towards a comprehensive evaluation of large language models in multilingual learning. In *Findings of the Association for Computational Linguistics: EMNLP 2023*, pages 13171–13189, Singapore. Association for Computational Linguistics.

Junyi Li, Tianyi Tang, Wayne Xin Zhao, Jian-Yun Nie, and Ji-Rong Wen. 2024. Pre-trained language models for text generation: A survey. *ACM Computing Surveys*, 56(9):1–39.

Timothy Liu and De Wen Soh. 2022. Towards better characterization of paraphrases. In *Proceedings of the 60th Annual Meeting of the Association for Computational Linguistics (Volume 1: Long Papers)*, pages 8592–8601, Dublin, Ireland. Association for Computational Linguistics.

Paul A Luce and David B Pisoni. 1998. Recognizing spoken words: The neighborhood activation model. *Ear and hearing*, 19(1):1.

Rachel McArdle and Richard H Wilson. 2008. Predicting word-recognition performance in noise by young listeners with normal hearing using acoustic, phonetic, and lexical variables. *Journal of the American Academy of Audiology*, 19(6):507–518.

AI Meta. 2024. Introducing meta llama 3: The most capable openly available llm to date. *Meta AI*.

George A Miller. 1947. The masking of speech. *Psychological bulletin*, 44(2):105.

Crystal Nakatsu and Michael White. 2006. Learning to say it well: Reranking realizations by predicted synthesis quality. In *Proceedings of the 21st International Conference on Computational Linguistics and 44th Annual Meeting of the Association for Computational Linguistics*, pages 1113–1120, Sydney, Australia. Association for Computational Linguistics.

OpenAI. 2023. Gpt-4 technical report. *Preprint*, arXiv:2303.08774.

Long Ouyang, Jeffrey Wu, Xu Jiang, Diogo Almeida, Carroll Wainwright, Pamela Mishkin, Chong Zhang, Sandhini Agarwal, Katarina Slama, Alex Ray, John Schulman, Jacob Hilton, Fraser Kelton, Luke Miller, Maddie Simens, Amanda Askell, Peter Welinder, Paul F Christiano, Jan Leike, and Ryan Lowe. 2022. Training language models to follow instructions with human feedback. In *Advances in Neural Information Processing Systems*, volume 35, pages 27730–27744. Curran Associates, Inc.

J. M. Pickett. 1957. Perception of vowels heard in noises of various spectra. *The JASA*, 29(5):613–620.

Dongqi Pu and Vera Demberg. 2023. ChatGPT vs human-authored text: Insights into controllable text summarization and sentence style transfer. In *Proceedings of the 61st Annual Meeting of the Association for Computational Linguistics (Volume 4: Student Research Workshop)*, pages 1–18, Toronto, Canada. Association for Computational Linguistics.

Alec Radford, Jeffrey Wu, Rewon Child, David Luan, Dario Amodei, Ilya Sutskever, et al. 2019. Language models are unsupervised multitask learners. *OpenAI blog*, 1(8):9.

Mirco Ravanelli, Titouan Parcollet, Peter Plantinga, Aku Rouhe, Samuele Cornell, Loren Lugosch, Cem Subakan, Nauman Dawalatabad, Abdelwahab Heba, Jianyuan Zhong, Ju-Chieh Chou, Sung-Lin Yeh, Szu-Wei Fu, Chien-Feng Liao, Elena Rastorgueva, François Grondin, William Aris, Hwidong Na, Yan Gao, Renato De Mori, and Yoshua Bengio. 2021. SpeechBrain: A general-purpose speech toolkit. *Preprint*, arXiv:2106.04624. ArXiv:2106.04624.

Victor Sanh, Lysandre Debut, Julien Chaumond, and Thomas Wolf. 2019. Distilbert, a distilled version of bert: smaller, faster, cheaper and lighter. *ArXiv*, abs/1910.01108.

Tim Schoof and Stuart Rosen. 2015. High sentence predictability increases the fluctuating masker benefit. *The JASA*, 138(3):EL181–EL186.

Jonathan Shen, Ruoming Pang, Ron J Weiss, Mike Schuster, Navdeep Jaitly, Zongheng Yang, Zhifeng Chen, Yu Zhang, Yuxuan Wang, Rj Skerrv-Ryan, et al. 2018. Natural tts synthesis by conditioning wavenet on mel spectrogram predictions. In *2018 IEEE international conference on acoustics, speech and signal processing (ICASSP)*, pages 4779–4783. IEEE.

Jiao Sun, Yufei Tian, Wangchunshu Zhou, Nan Xu, Qian Hu, Rahul Gupta, John Wieting, Nanyun Peng, and Xuezhe Ma. 2023a. Evaluating large language models on controlled generation tasks. In *Proceedings of the 2023 Conference on Empirical Methods in Natural Language Processing*, pages 3155–3168, Singapore. Association for Computational Linguistics.

Jiao Sun, Yufei Tian, Wangchunshu Zhou, Nan Xu, Qian Hu, Rahul Gupta, John Wieting, Nanyun Peng, and Xuezhe Ma. 2023b. Evaluating large language models on controlled generation tasks. In *Proceedings of the 2023 Conference on Empirical Methods in Natural Language Processing*, pages 3155–3168, Singapore. Association for Computational Linguistics.

Mirac Suzgun, Luke Melas-Kyriazi, and Dan Jurafsky. 2022. Prompt-and-rerank: A method for zero-shot and few-shot arbitrary textual style transfer with small language models. In *Proceedings of the 2022 Conference on Empirical Methods in Natural Language Processing*, pages 2195–2222, Abu Dhabi, United Arab Emirates. Association for Computational Linguistics.

Cees H Taal, Richard C Hendriks, Richard Heusdens, and Jesper Jensen. 2010. A short-time objective intelligibility measure for time-frequency weighted noisy speech. In *2010 IEEE ICASSP*, pages 4214–4217.

Genichi Taguchi. 1986. *Introduction to quality engineering: designing quality into products and processes*.

Yan Tang and Martin Cooke. 2016. Glimpse-Based Metrics for Predicting Speech Intelligibility in Additive Noise Conditions. In *Proc. Interspeech 2016*, pages 2488–2492.

Verena Uslar, Esther Ruigendijk, Cornelia Hamann, Thomas Brand, and Birger Kollmeier. 2011. How does linguistic complexity influence intelligibility in a german audiometric sentence intelligibility test? *International Journal of Audiology*, 50(9):621–631.

Verena N Uslar, Rebecca Carroll, Mirko Hanke, Cornelia Hamann, Esther Ruigendijk, Thomas Brand, and Birger Kollmeier. 2013. Development and evaluation of a linguistically and audiologically controlled sentence intelligibility test. *The JASA*, 134(4):3039–3056.

Cassia Valentini-Botinhao and Mirjam Wester. 2014. Using linguistic predictability and the lombard effect to increase the intelligibility of synthetic speech in noise. In *Proc. Interspeech 2014*, pages 2063–2067.

Eline C van Knijff, Martine Coene, and Paul J Govaerts. 2018. Speech understanding in noise in elderly adults: the effect of inhibitory control and syntactic complexity. *International journal of language & communication disorders*, 53(3):628–642.

Andrew Varga and Herman JM Steeneken. 1993. Assessment for automatic speech recognition: Ii. noisex-92: A database and an experiment to study the effect of additive noise on speech recognition systems. *Speech communication*, 12(3):247–251.

Andrea Weber and Roel Smits. 2003. Consonant and vowel confusion patterns by american english listeners. In *15th International Congress of Phonetic Sciences [ICPhS 2003]*.

Jason Wei, Maarten Bosma, Vincent Zhao, Kelvin Guu, Adams Wei Yu, Brian Lester, Nan Du, Andrew M. Dai, and Quoc V Le. 2022. Finetuned language models are zero-shot learners. In *International Conference on Learning Representations*.

Jason Weston, Emily Dinan, and Alexander Miller. 2018. Retrieve and refine: Improved sequence generation models for dialogue. In *Proceedings of the 2018 EMNLP Workshop SCAI: The 2nd International Workshop on Search-Oriented Conversational AI*, pages 87–92, Brussels, Belgium. Association for Computational Linguistics.

Richard H Wilson and Wendy B Cates. 2008. A comparison of two word-recognition tasks in multitalker babble: Speech recognition in noise test (sprint) and words-in-noise test (win). *Journal of the American Academy of Audiology*, 19(7):548–556.

Xianjun Yang, Yan Li, Xinlu Zhang, Haifeng Chen, and Wei Cheng. 2023. Exploring the limits of chatgpt for query or aspect-based text summarization. *arXiv preprint arXiv:2302.08081*.

Hanqing Zhang, Haolin Song, Shaoyu Li, Ming Zhou, and Dawei Song. 2023. A survey of controllable text generation using transformer-based pre-trained language models. *ACM Computing Surveys*, 56(3):1–37.

Mengqiu Zhang, Petko Nikolov Petkov, and W Bastiaan Kleijn. 2013. Rephrasing-based speech intelligibility enhancement. In *INTERSPEECH*, pages 3587–3591.

Tianyi Zhang, Varsha Kishore, Felix Wu, Kilian Q. Weinberger, and Yoav Artzi. 2020. Bertscore: Evaluating text generation with bert. In *International Conference on Learning Representations*.

Wenhao Zhu, Hongyi Liu, Qingxiu Dong, Jingjing Xu, Shujian Huang, Lingpeng Kong, Jiajun Chen, and Lei Li. 2023. Multilingual machine translation with large language models: Empirical results and analysis. *Preprint*, arXiv:2304.04675.

A Definitions

Babble Noise. It is one of the most commonly occurring noise types in the real world (Miller, 1947). Typically, it is the noise that exists in a cafeteria or other crowded environments, wherein individuals engage in conversations in the backdrop of other conversations. The simultaneous speech produced by several individuals in the background masks the target speech and could hinder listening. The babble noise in the NOISEX-92 database that we use in this work is a recording of 100 people speaking in a canteen (Varga and Steeneken, 1993; Deshpande and Holambe, 2009).

Signal-to-Noise Ratio. To measure the noise level, a commonly used metric is the signal-to-noise ratio (SNR) (Taguchi, 1986). SNR represents the ratio of the power of a clean (undistorted) signal and a noise signal, which are combined to form the distorted signal. Simply put, it is a fraction of powers as defined in Equation (1). It is commonly measured on a logarithmic scale and referred to in units of decibels (dB), as defined in Equation (2). The power of a signal is the sum of the absolute squares of signal magnitudes averaged across the time domain.

$$SNR = \frac{P_{signal}}{P_{noise}} \quad (1)$$

$$\begin{aligned} SNR_{dB} &= 10 \log_{10}(SNR) \\ &= 10 \log_{10}(\frac{P_{signal}}{P_{noise}}) \end{aligned} \quad (2)$$

When a clean speech signal is mixed with a noise signal with equal power, the SNR of the resultant distorted speech is 0 dB. Similarly, when the power of the clean signal is higher than that of the noise, the SNR of the resultant signal is positive (> 0 dB). Higher SNR scores indicate better audibility. On the other hand, when the noise power is more in the processed signal, the SNR value is negative (< 0 dB).

B More Samples from the PiN Dataset

In Table 8, we provide more paraphrase triplets from the PiN dataset.

C Absolute Scores

We provide absolute scores for different evaluation metrics in Table 5 in addition to their pairwise ratios.

Prompt-ID	PhLen	PPL	STOI
$p_{zsl-low}$	50.67	159.95	0.570
$p_{zsl-med}$	42.08	165.56	0.569
$p_{zsl-high}$	46.68	193.85	0.577
$p_{pas_{(n=6)}}$	44.67	182.77	0.617
$p_{pas_{(n=12)}}$	44.88	184.52	0.627
p_{icl}	47.27	146.71	0.573
`{input text}`	38.02	236.65	0.577

Table 5: Absolute scores for utterance length (PhLen), linguistic predictability (PPL), and acoustic intelligibility (STOI) of `{input text}` and generated outputs by different prompts.

D In-context Learning

Prior research has shown that LLMs can efficiently learn to control text generation with demonstrations and perform better than just providing a task description (Brown et al., 2020). Thus for the in-context learning (ICL) setup, the input prompt is modified to include a set of exemplars that represent the desired model behavior. In other words, to instruct the model to generate acoustically intelligible paraphrases in an ICL setting requires a set of sentences and their corresponding paraphrases that are acoustically more intelligible in a noise condition.

To provide the best in-context demonstrations, we created another set of 300 short sentences from the Switchboard corpus excluding those in the evaluation set. Then, their corresponding paraphrases were generated by prompting ChatGPT with $p_{zsl-med}$. Following speech synthesis and noise mixing with babble noise at SNR -5 dB, we identified the top 5 pairs that exhibited a larger pairwise difference in STOI scores. Further, the sentences within each pair were rearranged in such a way that the second sentence is always better intelligible than its paired paraphrase. Further, the sentences within each demonstration pair were concatenated with a token (eg: '=>') and embedded with $p_{zsl-low}$ for in-context learning. Table 6 represents the exact prompt statement (p_{icl}) that we used for the in-context learning.

Results and Analysis As shown in Table 7, the model learned to generate paraphrases, similar to those given as examples. Compared to the zero-shot learning with minimal task description ($p_{zsl-low}$), the model in the ICL setup (p_{icl}) gener-

Prompt-ID	Prompt
p_{icl}	Look at the samples of a sentence and its intelligible paraphrase: 1. *I don't know if you are familiar with that.* => *I have no idea if you're familiar with that.* 2. *what other long-range goals do you have besides college?* => *Apart from college, what are your other long-term objectives?* 3. *I don't have access either. Although, I did at one time* => *In the past, I had access, but currently, I don't.* 4. *Right now I've got it narrowed down to the top four teams.* => *At this point, I've trimmed my options and picked 4 top teams.* 5. *prohibition didn't stop it and didn't do anything really.* => *It continued despite the prohibition, which didn't accomplish anything.* Similarly, generate an **intelligible** paraphrase for the input sentence: `{input text}`

Table 6: The prompt used for the in-context learning setup.

Prompt-ID	STS↑	LD↑	*PWR*-PhLen↓	*PWR*-PPL↓	*PWR*-STOI ↑
p_{icl}	0.872	0.627	1.250*	0.947	0.997

Table 7: An evaluation of the ICL setup. LLM fails to improve acoustic intelligibility (*PWR*-STOI < 1.0), though it learns to capture the demonstrated textual attributes like lexical deviation and predictability.

ated texts that are semantically more similar and lexically less divergent from the input sentences. More interestingly, the model also learned to optimize the desired textual attributes like length (*PWR*-PhLen) and linguistic predictability (*PWR*-PPL) of generated paraphrases, even in the absence of prompt tokens to explicitly control those features. Nevertheless, the **demonstrations are still not helpful in controlling the non-textual attribute**. We observed that the acoustic intelligibility scores of output sentences were *not significantly* different from their input sentences (*PWR*-STOI = 0.997). Once again, this shows the inability of the LLM to generate acoustically intelligible paraphrases, even though it captures textual attributes from the given exemplars.

Sentence_ID	Sentence
s_1	they give more information than opinions
s_2	they seem to give more of just the facts than opinions
s_3	they seem to give more facts than opinions
s_1	you don't hear much about it in the big ones
s_2	in the big ones you don't hear about it
s_3	you never hear about it really in the big ones
s_1	I think we talked for a good eight minutes about the subject
s_2	we talked for about eight minutes
s_3	I think we talked for about eight minutes
s_1	I like having people over for dinner
s_2	I enjoy having people over for dinner
s_3	if I have people over for dinner I like it to be
s_1	I studied every piece of material I could
s_2	I studied every part of the material
s_3	and studied every bit of material that I could study
s_1	I wanted to be a teacher at one time
s_2	at one point I wanted to be a teacher
s_3	I thought at one time I wanted to be a teacher
s_1	they never imagined it would be a hit
s_2	in fact, they never thought it would be a hit
s_3	they never expected it to be a hit
s_1	they want a lot more men to participate
s_2	they need more men to participate
s_3	they really looking for a lot more men to participate
s_1	we gave them about seven minutes
s_2	we gave them about seven minutes according to my watch
s_3	they were given seven minutes
s_1	you don't hear much about it in the big ones
s_2	in the big ones you don't hear about it
s_3	you never hear about it really in the big ones
s_1	at that stage of life you only have so much money left
s_2	you only have a limited amount of money left
s_3	you only have so much money left at that point in your life
s_1	I was angry that they were capable of doing that
s_2	I was mad that they could do that
s_3	I was just pissed as hell that they could do that

Table 8: A list of paraphrase triplets (s_1, s_2, s_3) from the PiN dataset. Sentences in each triplet are arranged in such a way that s_1 is acoustically less intelligible than s_2, and acoustically more intelligible than s_3, in a listening condition with babble noise at SNR -5 dB.

Human-Centered Design Recommendations for LLM-as-a-Judge

Qian Pan
Qian.Pan@ibm.com
IBM Research
Cambridge, MA, USA

Zahra Ashktorab
zahra.ashktorab1@ibm.com
IBM Research
Yorktown Heights, NY, USA

Michael Desmond
mdesmond@us.ibm.com
IBM Research
Yorktown Heights, NY, USA

Martin Santillan Cooper
msantillancooper@ibm.com
IBM Research
Capital Federal, Argentina

James Johnson
jmjohnson@us.ibm.com
IBM Research
Cambridge, MA, USA

Rahul Nair
rahul.nair@ie.ibm.com
IBM Research
Mulhuddart, Dublin, Ireland

Elizabeth Daly
elizabeth.daly@ie.ibm.com
IBM Research
Mulhuddart, Dublin, Ireland

Werner Geyer
werner.geyer@us.ibm.com
IBM Research
Cambridge, MA, USA

Abstract

Traditional reference-based metrics, such as BLEU and ROUGE, are less effective for assessing outputs from Large Language Models (LLMs) that produce highly creative or superior-quality text, or in situations where reference outputs are unavailable. While human evaluation remains an option, it is costly and difficult to scale. Recent work using LLMs as evaluators (LLM-as-a-judge) is promising, but trust and reliability remain a significant concern. Integrating human input is crucial to ensure criteria used to evaluate are aligned with the human's intent, and evaluations are robust and consistent. This paper presents a user study of a design exploration called EvaluLLM, that enables users to leverage LLMs as customizable judges, promoting human involvement to balance trust and cost-saving potential with caution. Through interviews with eight domain experts, we identified the need for assistance in developing effective evaluation criteria aligning the LLM-as-a-judge with practitioners' preferences and expectations. We offer findings and design recommendations to optimize human-assisted LLM-as-judge systems.

1 Introduction

Recent advancements in Large Language Models (LLMs) challenge traditional methods of assessing natural language generation (NLG) quality, as known metrics, such as BLEU (Papineni et al., 2002) and ROUGE (Lin, 2004), fall short for creative tasks. The diverse and expanding capabilities of LLMs (Liang et al., 2022) present a selection challenge for practitioners, requiring evaluations of extensive outputs across contexts like summarization and retrieval-augmented generation (RAG). The subjective and use case-specific nature of emerging NLG tasks often demands human review, making the evaluation process hard to scale without suitable automatic metrics. While experts can perform evaluations, this is costly and impractical for rapid iteration in early development stages. (Gehrmann et al., 2023).

One potential solution to these challenges is to leverage the capabilities of LLMs to aid in the evaluation process. Despite not always being accurate, LLMs have the potential to significantly reduce the workload by identifying outputs where they are not confident, thus indicating where human input may be required. Additionally, LLMs can assist practitioners in identifying and customizing criteria specific to their use case—such as, for example, faithfulness to contextual information, naturalness of the conversation, and succinctness—with which they wish to conduct their evaluations. This customization enables a more targeted and effective assessment of model outputs, tailored to the specific requirements of their tasks. In this paper, we present results from a user study of EvaluLLM (Desmond et al., 2024), a tool designed to facilitate the evaluation of model outputs. EvaluLLM simplifies how practitioners choose LLMs by offering a quick way to assess and compare their performance across various tasks. This method accelerates the

Proceedings of the 1st Human-Centered Large Language Modeling Workshop, pages 16–29
August 15, 2024 ©2024 Association for Computational Linguistics

development of evaluation criteria and helps manage the growing variety and capabilities of LLMs.

To understand the challenges and user needs in model evaluation that leverage LLM-as-a-Judge to automate the process, we conducted formative, semi-structured interviews with 8 practitioners (data scientists, software engineers, and AI engineers) who have been involved in model performance evaluation projects over the past year. Our interviews revealed various challenges and needs. For instance, practitioners highlighted the necessity for rapid performance comparison across different setups, the importance of defining evaluation criteria (e.g., structured and customizable templates aligned with specific use cases), and strategies for effectively integrating LLM-as-a-Judge into their workflow (e.g., starting with a small subset of data before scaling up). In this paper, we present the following contributions:

- We describe EvaluLLM (Desmond et al., 2024), an LLM-Assisted evaluation tool that enables users to select multiple models, define custom metrics for NLG evaluation, and review the results while providing feedback to observe the agreement between human and AI evaluations.
- We present qualitative findings from interviews with domain experts (N = 8) revealing challenges and user needs for model evaluation workflows including LLM-as-a-judge.
- We make design recommendations and provide example feature designs to enable users to define criteria interactively, ensuring transparent and rapid access to LLM-as-a-judge's preferences while balancing trade-offs across multiple dimensions in a self-consistent manner.

2 Related work

LLMs trained to follow instructions can generate results that surpass the quality of data produced by humans. This makes it increasingly challenging to assess the quality of natural language generation (NLG) outputs (Liang et al., 2022) (Xiao et al., 2023) (Liu et al., 2023b). Traditional reference-based metrics, such as ROUGE (Lin, 2004) and BLEU (Papineni et al., 2002), might not effectively capture the essence of LLM outputs, especially in scenarios where the output space is broad and varied. This means multiple different outcomes can all be valid, making it nearly impossible to create sufficiently comprehensive reference sets. Consequently, these metrics may not be reliable indicators of NLG output quality, as they often demonstrate a low correlation with human judgments (Freitag et al., 2022).

Recent advances highlight LLMs' potential as customizable judges, (Liu et al., 2023a) (Wang et al., 2023a) (Zheng et al., 2023) capable of adapting to various tasks beyond traditional evaluation methods. Techniques like G-Eval (Liu et al., 2023a) use chain-of-thought prompting and form-filling to assess NLG quality, while GPTScore (Fu et al., 2023) evaluates using conditional token probabilities, enhancing scoring granularity. AlpacaEval (Li et al., 2023) (Yuan et al., 2024) compares model win rates, and Prometheus (Kim et al., 2023a) is a fine-tuned LLM specifically designed for evaluation tasks. These methods align closely with human preferences, especially in creative tasks, emphasizing LLMs' ability to mimic human judgment. Their effectiveness relies on tailored prompt design and user-defined criteria for precise evaluations. While not part of this paper, in our own work, we have also done comprehensive benchmarking of human agreement of different LLM-as-a-judge approaches for different use cases and we found that depending on use case, LLMs as judges, and judging approach, we were able to achieve good results. Note that this is often a hard problem for humans too and inter-rater reliability can be a good reference.

Previous research has investigated using expert-labeled data to develop custom evaluation metrics like AUTOCALIBRATE (Liu et al., 2023b), but this method is limited by the availability of such data. For reference-free evaluations, interactive human involvement is preferable, allowing users to refine criteria effectively by reviewing outputs. ConstitutionMaker (Petridis et al., 2023) enables feedback on model outputs to iteratively refine prompts, focusing more on AI prototyping than evaluation. Other tools like Zeno (Cabrera et al., 2023), the What-If Tool (Wexler et al., 2019), and Errudite (Wu et al., 2019) help identify model vulnerabilities by analyzing specific data segments. EvalLM (Kim et al., 2023b) allows users to define criteria interactively, using LLM-as-a-judges for output ratings, although this can be limited by LLM reasoning capabilities (Zheng et al., 2023). Our study builds on these insights, proposing a system where practitioners define criteria in natural language for LLMs to perform pairwise comparisons, enhancing trust through a "human-in-the-loop" blind review process that eliminates the need for expert data.

3 EvaluLLM

To explore how to support users in developing their own custom evaluation criteria for accurate and reliable evaluations that align with human preferences in a trustworthy manner, we designed and deployed EvaluLLM (Desmond et al., 2024). This tool enables users to generate evaluation outputs by providing a prompt, selecting multiple models, and defining LLM-as-a-Judge with custom metrics using natural language. Users can then review the results and provide feedback, inspecting the agreement between human and AI evaluations through a blind review process. In this paper, we use EvaluLLM as a conceptual design probe with users to explore the design space of how to support development of custom evaluation criteria for accurate and reliable evaluations that align with human preferences in a trustworthy manner.

The overall user flow of EvaluLLM comprises of three stages (see Figure 1). The build experience focuses on defining the LLM-assisted evaluation experience to initiate the auto-evaluation process, the review experience, providing a high-level summary of the evaluation results, and the inspect experience allows users to manually examine the generated outputs through a blind review process. The data generated from this process can be used to calculate the agreement rate, assisting practitioners in better assessing the agreement between human and LLM-as-a-judges. This assessment is crucial for calibrating trust and aids in making informed decisions about whether to change configurations and rerun the evaluation.

In the absence of reference data, related studies suggest that LLMs may not be entirely suitable for use as numerical judges (Zheng et al., 2023). This is because grading based on single answers may fail to detect minor distinctions between specific pairs. Furthermore, the outcomes could become unreliable, as absolute scores tend to vary more than relative pairwise results when there are changes in the judging model (Zheng et al., 2023). To mitigate these challenges, EvaluLLM uses a pairwise comparison approach, as it can reduce the complexity of the evaluation task by breaking down the comparison of multiple outputs into smaller decisions between pairs of data which might yield to more accurate evaluation results at the cost of additional inference operations. The evaluation method involves making pairwise comparisons between the outputs of different models, similar to the AlpacaEval approach (Li et al., 2023). However, instead of comparing outputs to a single reference, they are compared against one another.

3.1 Build

The build experience (see Figure 1) includes two major components: the Generator (Figure 1A) and the Evaluator (Figure 1B). The Generator section (Figure 1A) is designed to produce evaluation data, supporting users in selecting a pre-uploaded dataset and inputting their task prompts. Users can incorporate data variables from the dataset's structure into the task prompt using the conventional curly bracket format. Additionally, the system provides a range of LLMs for users to choose from for the purpose of performance evaluation. The Evaluator section (Figure 1B) is where users can choose the LLM-as-a-judge model for automatic evaluation and specify the custom metrics that the judge will use to assess the outputs from the generator. This initial version of EvaluLLM, deliberately provides only a freeform input box to support maximum creativity, as the aim was to gain more insights into the types of inputs users would provide to define criteria in natural language and the kind of support users might need to define custom metrics. Once the user completes the setup, they can click the "Run Evaluation" button to initiate the evaluation.

3.2 Review

Upon completion of the automatic evaluation, results are available for review. Users can view a high-level performance summary and a detailed results table. The summary includes a model leader board (Figure 1C), ranking selected LLMs by their win rates derived from evaluated output pairs. The performance visualization (Figure 1D) shows detailed win-loss statistics for each model based on pairwise comparisons by the LLM-as-a-judge. Additionally, the agreement rate (Figure 1E) indicates the alignment between human and LLM-as-judges, helping users gauge the reliability of evaluations. This feature becomes available after users manually rate output samples.

3.3 Inspect

Users can examine auto-evaluation results through two main methods. First, users can conduct a blind review, manually inspecting data to assess

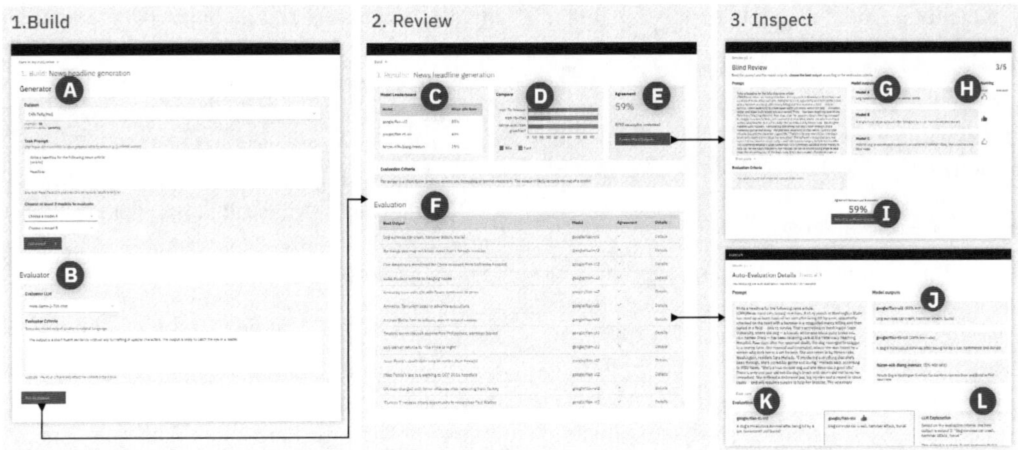

Figure 1: EvaluLLM interfaces and key features

the reliability of LLM evaluations (Figure 1G). In this process, models' names are hidden to prevent bias, and users select the best output from all presented outputs. Ratings from this process are used to calculate an agreement score, which measures alignment between user and LLM-as-a-judge preferences (Figure 1E, I). After rating, users can view model identities and the updated agreement score (Figure 1H, I), providing insight into the effectiveness of the evaluation criteria. Users can also access detailed results on the review page, which displays the LLM-as-a-Judge's aggregated rankings and win rates from pairwise comparisons (Figure 1J). Evaluation rationales are provided next to each comparison result (Figure 1L, K), helping users decide whether to trust the results or adjust settings for a reevaluation.

4 Methodology

Our goal was to explore the challenges users encounter during LLM-assisted model evaluations and, based on our observations, to design a framework that meets their needs and supports effective collaboration between humans and LLM-as-a-judges. We used EvaluLLM to facilitate the creation of evaluation tasks and conducted our research through semi-structured interviews using Webex. Participants accessed a prototype of EvaluLLM, shared their screens, and used think-aloud methods to create evaluation tasks. Each participant worked on the same task: using an LLM-as-a-judge to identify the best model for generating headlines from the CNN/Daily Mail dataset.

4.1 Participants

We recruited 8 industry professionals (Appendix Table 1) with deep domain knowledge in model evaluation at a large technology company (2 females and 6 males) via social media recruiting, with participation and recommendations from various individuals. These industry professionals primarily consist of data scientists, software engineers, and AI engineers. Eligible participants were those who had hands-on experience evaluating large language model performance in their projects in the past year. The interviews were conducted remotely, and participants volunteered and consented to the recording of the session, as well as to the use of the interview results for research purposes.

4.2 Data Analysis

Two authors independently reviewed the transcripts from recorded video sessions to pinpoint users' needs, system shortcomings, and challenges in the evaluation workflow. This independent review helped minimize bias and allowed for a comprehensive data exploration. Each author used a codebook of example quotes to support the identified themes. The authors then met to merge similar themes and address any initially missed, resulting in three main categories: use case challenges, evaluation criteria, and evaluation workflow, detailed in Appendix Table 2. This classification captures the complexities of the evaluation process, encompassing users' needs, system limitations, and evaluative challenges.

5 Results

Our data analysis identified nine themes, categorized into use case challenges, evaluation criteria, and evaluation workflow (for a full list with example quotes see Table 2 in the Appendix).

5.1 Use Case Challenges

The system requires users to input a prompt for their specific task, after which it generates the output and proceeds with the evaluation. This approach involves sending the identical prompt to various models for output evaluation. However, this methodology poses limitations for experienced users who tailor prompts for specific models, such as LLaMA. Our participants described instances of **absence of specifications** where clients lack clarity on the task's data requirements.

Additionally, there are numerous open-source and closed-source LLM models available, and users would like to test various setups, e.g., model selections, model configurations, and prompts. They would like the system to **support comparison with different setups.** Given time constraints and limited investment resources, it is often impractical to test all models with their use case data. Teams usually begin with top-performing models, either from public benchmarks close to their use case or chosen based on their well-known reputation. Model selection is transient and highly constrained by project requirements. Instead of evaluating multiple models' performance with different prompts, they typically start with 1-2 models and improve performance through prompt engineering. This involves running the model with various prompts and parameter settings, where they often iterate over the setup to match specific baseline performance. It requires rapid performance comparison and support for evaluation data, accommodating multiple models and considering combinations with different setups.

Shifting evaluation priority often occurs as the project progresses. At the beginning of the project, where the main purpose is often the proof of concept for a specific proposed solution, the evaluation focus is mainly around feasibility testing. This involves assessing whether the proposed system or solution can produce accurate answers. However, as the project progresses into production, the evaluation purpose might shift from rapid model performance comparison to continual improvement with user feedback, performance monitoring, and reporting potential issues to draw developers' attentions. As evaluation priorities might differ for various use cases in different project phases, when designing an LLM-as-a-Judge solution, shared needs among these different phases and unique requirements in each phase need to be clearly articulated. This could help better define and design the experience and interaction to effectively support the diverse requirements for each phase.

5.2 Evaluation Criteria

We identified several themes related to how users developed, changed, and trusted the evaluation criteria they were working with. While participants appreciated the flexibility of using the freeform approach in EvaluLLM, many expressed that they **desire structured and customizable templates** for specific use cases that can be tweaked for their purposes. They believe such templates would help them start with an evaluation baseline.

Moreover, participants highlighted the necessity of distinct evaluation criteria for various tasks. For example, they noted that a RAG task might require one set of criteria, while a creative task might demand another. Participants often crafted criteria complete with descriptions and scoring. One typical approach involved naming each criterion, defining it, and then assigning a score.

Evaluation criteria serve as a medium to communicate user preferences to the model. An effective criterion not only needs to reflect the user's preferences but also must function well to enable the model to understand and follow instructions. When reflecting on evaluation criteria, participants expressed the **need for multiple rounds of iterations** when refining their criteria. *"It can be really hard to figure out how to express the evaluation criteria in a way that makes sense to the model. But it can also just be hard in your own mind to figure out what it means for a title to be good."* P2

The importance of giving supporting multiple rounds to refine and expand criteria emerged when looking at the types of dimensions participants created. We found that users tend to prioritize more objective metrics such as accuracy before they start to consider the styling of the outcome. At the beginning of the project, the primary concern for a client is getting the correct answer from the model. That is not to say, that our participants did not care about more subjective criteria, but that happens later in the process.

Although users might have a rough idea of what

they want, it is challenging to describe everything at the beginning, especially when they don't have access to the evaluation data. One participant struggled during the criteria definition process as he was required to define the criteria before he could see the output data. Providing the output might help users articulate what they want or don't want, assisting them in iterating the criteria description or adding examples to better align with their preferences.

Users express a desire for more than just a high-level result summary; they are keen on obtaining a detailed breakdown of each dimension and a need for the system to **display performance for each criteria individually**. EvaluLLM currently only presents a win rate as a high-level performance summary metric to showcase the winning model on the leaderboard. Participants expressed the desire to view performance across each dimension rather than a high level win-rate.

5.3 Evaluation Workflow

While presenting the tool to users, we probed them on their current evaluation workflows and how they would imagine incorporating EvaluLLM. Users expressed the challenges they faced when doing manual evaluations and how they would use automated methods and the EvaluLLM experience to address those challenges. Although there are only 10 examples in our testing dataset, generating the evaluation results after user created the evaluation is time consuming because of calls to the model. Model calls are expensive and time consuming and one potential way to address this is to **run the evaluation on a subset of the data first**.

To evaluate the agreement of the LLM-as-a-Judge preferences with humans, participants were asked to conduct blind reviews of the model's output. These reviews would be utilized to calculate the agreement between the LLM-as-a-judge and the participants. While it is beneficial to observe the agreement rate in the summary page, users also desire more control over the workflow and seek instant feedback during the manual review process. They would like to see how much the LLM-as-a-judge agrees with them once they provide feedback and wish for the system to proactively provide criteria modification suggestions. One way of providing **instant feedback on human-AI agreement** is to allow users to either initially upload human evaluations for comparison with the automatic evaluations. Another way is to conduct a blind review before the evaluations are presented, ensuring that users receive instant feedback on human-AI agreement as soon as the evaluations are ready.

During testing, we observed that some participants might provide overly detailed instructions for both the task prompt and the evaluation criteria. The design intention was to simplify the user input requirements, seeking only the evaluation criteria rather than a complete evaluation prompt with detailed evaluation process. However, some participants included the step-by-step evaluation process in the criteria definition input. Additionally, some participants inquired about adjusting their evaluations per judge.

As our participants are domain experts in model evaluation, they are well aware of potential biases in the model. They actively seek transparency regarding the bias mitigation strategy to effectively calibrate their trust in LLM-as-a-Judge results. Additionally, participants were cognizant of self-enhancement bias (Zheng et al., 2023) and expressed concerns about the LLM-as-a-judge being one of the models to be evaluated. **Ensuring transparency for trustworthy evaluation** was deemed crucial by users, such as transparency concerning the prompts sent to the judge and whether bias mitigation has been implemented. One user remarked, *"It seems like Granite always displays first, and Flan-UL-2 always comes second. Does the system randomly switch positions?" P5*

5.4 Limitations

Our study is based on a small sample of only 8 domain experts, potentially impacting the generalizability of our findings. In addition, our methodology primarily concentrated on observing users utilizing our specific evaluation tool with one predefined dataset. This approach may restrict the broader applicability of our results. Note that EvaluLLM at the time of this study was a functioning proof-of-concept but not yet a scalable systems that can be deployed to a large user population. However, we believe our findings still offer relevant insights into the challenges and needs users encounter when using LLM-as-a-Judge tools, as evidenced by our focused line of questioning aimed at understanding how more automated evaluations integrate into users' workflows.

6 Discussion and Design Recommendations

Our findings highlight user needs across different use cases when using LLM-as-a-judge. Users require guidance to evaluate model outputs effectively. We discuss the implications of our findings and propose design recommendations for LLM-as-a-judge tools and user experiences.

6.1 Efficient Criteria Iteration

LLMs can generate high-quality outputs aligned with human preferences, but processing the entire dataset is costly and time-consuming, especially with methods like pairwise comparisons, which increase compute costs significantly. To optimize efficiency, it's advisable to start a project by allowing users to refine their evaluation criteria using a representative data sample before scaling up to the full dataset (see Figure 2). Effective sampling enhances learning for LLM-as-a-Judge by selecting diverse and representative outputs. Techniques like clustering (Chang et al., 2021) or graph-based search (Su et al., 2022) can aid in output selection for human evaluation. Addressing misalignments and manually reviewing low-confidence outputs (Desmond et al., 2021) are crucial, as is displaying a subset of evaluations to lessen users' cognitive load and facilitate iterative refinement of evaluation criteria.

6.2 Structured and Customizable Templates

For creative generation tasks, it's crucial to employ diverse, custom criteria. To streamline this process, we propose providing standard criteria that are universally applicable across various use cases, supplemented by customizable templates. As illustrated in our design explorations (see Appendix Figure 3), users can select from predefined criteria dimensions (Figure 3A) or utilize recommended templates for common scenarios (Figure 3B). These templates are designed to be flexible, allowing easy adaptation to specific user needs.

Further enhancing customization, the proposed templates support hierarchical organization (see Appendix Figure 4), enabling the addition of new criteria dimensions (Figure 4G), nesting of subcriteria (Figure 4F), and removal of unwanted elements (Figure 4H). Users can also adjust scoring scales (Figure 4E). This hierarchical structure, supported by findings from related works (Zheng et al., 2023) (Kim et al., 2023c) (Stureborg et al., 2023), allows users to start with broad criteria and refine them to capture specific task nuances. To foster ongoing improvement and reuse, the system should enable users to save and share these templates (Figure 4B). Considering the benefits of balanced evaluations, users should be able to adjust the weight of different criteria dimensions, aligning more closely with human preferences. The inclusion of reference examples within the templates (Figure 4D) can further refine the criteria based on actual output data, enhancing the preference agreement process. This approach not only makes the criteria definition process more efficient but also ensures consistency and rigor in evaluating creative tasks, leading to more accurate and effective assessments.

Providing structured and customizable templates will not only expedite the process of criteria definition but also foster consistency and rigor in the evaluation of creative generation tasks, which will contribute to more accurate and effective evaluations.

6.3 Interactive Criteria Iteration

Our findings revealed crafting effective criteria typically requires multiple iterations. Criteria components such as name, definition, scale, and examples often need definition and refinement as users evaluate outputs. Users include examples of both poor and excellent outputs to help LLM-as-Judges distinguish quality through few-shot learning techniques. Related work (Kim et al., 2023c) indicates that users often develop new criteria during evaluations. To facilitate this process, a real-time feedback system that allows users to immediately see the impact of criteria modifications would be useful. Additionally, a user-friendly interface that enables easy modification and experimentation with criteria could significantly improve the efficiency and customization of the evaluation process.

6.4 Ensure Consistency

As human preferences may not be consistent within the same set, aligning with frequently changing preferences becomes a challenge. A self-consistency check mechanism can expedite this alignment. When refining criteria, any discrepancies between human and LLM-as-a-Judge evaluations should prompt a review of similar sample data post-calibration. Incorporating an automated consistency checker that flags potential criteria conflicts or inconsistencies could streamline the evaluation process by offering actionable solutions to

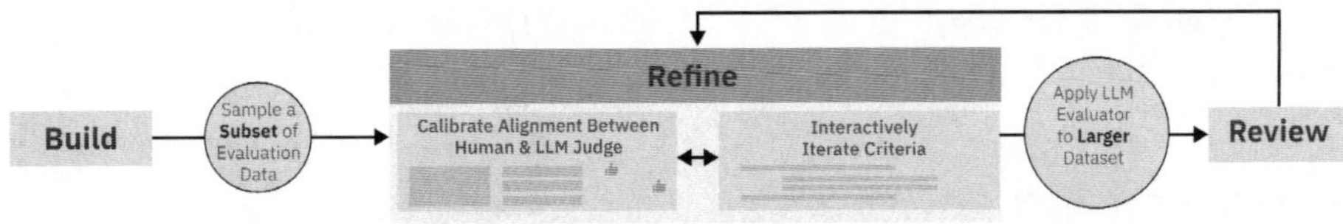

Figure 2: Recommended evaluation workflow: interactive refinement of criteria with a subset of data prior to applying evaluation to entire dataset can potentially improve preference alignment and trust calibration.

address these inconsistencies. Leveraging the diversity of logical paths in complex reasoning tasks, as suggested by recent studies (Stanovich and West, 2000), the self-consistency CoT method (Wang et al., 2023b) can generate multiple reasoning paths, selecting the most consistent answers by averaging over these paths, thus improving evaluation outcomes.

6.5 Support Different Setups

Our findings emphasize the need for an LLM to function flexibly as a judging system throughout different project phases. It should support a variety of evaluation data configurations, including diverse model selections, prompts, and settings. While some evaluations may only compare outputs from a specific prompt and model setting, optimal performance often requires tailored prompts and settings for each model, involving substantial prompt engineering and comparison of different configurations. Thus, the system must not only evaluate common settings across various models but also assess various prompts and settings for select models, highlighting the importance of designing an adaptable LLM judging system.

6.6 Adaptable Reference-Based Evaluation

Our user study findings showed that users often start projects without clear objectives, resulting in evaluations lacking reference data. Users interacting with the LLM-as-a-Judge system gradually accumulate reference data, either directly or from external sources, so it could be beneficial to design systems that incorporate human input to refine preference correspondence using expert-labeled data (Liu et al., 2023b) or other collected references. This flexible approach enhances the system's effectiveness and trustworthiness, ensuring it evolves in line with user preferences.

6.7 Enhance System Transparency

Our findings indicate that users value transparency to comprehend the LLM's role as a judge. This encompasses access to essential details like the specific prompt used (illustrated in Figure 5A) and the implementation of bias mitigation strategies. To design an effective LLM-as-a-Judge system, it is critical to make such information readily available. This can be facilitated by allowing users to view the prompt, enabling the system to explain evaluation results, and integrating visualization tools that demonstrate how user inputs affect the evaluation process.

6.8 Proactively Mitigate Potential Bias

Considering the persistent challenge of bias, systems should implement bias mitigation strategies that include swapping answer order to reduce position bias (Zheng et al., 2023) and treating inconsistent results as ties, or by randomly assigning positions in large datasets (Li et al., 2023) (Zheng et al., 2023). For verbosity bias, the "repetitive list" attack technique (Zheng et al., 2023) challenges LLMs to favor clarity over length in responses. Furthermore, enhancing LLMs' abilities in mathematical and reasoning tasks can be achieved through Chain-of-Thought approaches (Wei et al., 2022), coupled with reference-guided evaluation where the LLM generates and then evaluates its own initial responses.

6.9 Explore Further Automation

Our study found that task prompts often contain criteria, suggesting the possibility of extracting them automatically for tailored guidelines. Related work also shows that users prefer automated prompt refinement over manual revisions (Kim et al., 2023c). Various suggestions(see Appendix Figure 5), such as rephrasing (Figure 5A), adding reference examples (Figure 5B), incorporating more scales (Figure 5C), and introducing additional dimensions (Figure 5D), could be proactively provided by the system for humans to review to further accelerate evaluation correspondence. While these areas show promise for further improving the efficiency of preference correspondence, considering the limitations of automation systems, it is essential to place humans in the loop to calibrate accuracy and trustworthiness.

7 Conclusion

We studied EvaluLLM, an AI-assisted tool utilizing LLMs alongside humans as judges for LLM-generated content. Our findings highlight the potential of LLMs as customizable judges and underscore the importance of interactive, transparent, and user-centered evaluation processes. Based on our findings, we offer design suggestions for practitioners that can help them build more effective , nuanced, adaptable, and user-friendly evaluation tools that meet diverse needs as compared to automated benchmarks. Inspired by our user research, we are currently in the process of rolling out an evolved AI-assisted evaluation tool to a larger user population to observe "usage in the wild."

References

Ángel Alexander Cabrera, Erica Fu, Donald Bertucci, Kenneth Holstein, Ameet Talwalkar, Jason I Hong, and Adam Perer. 2023. Zeno: An interactive framework for behavioral evaluation of machine learning. In *Proceedings of the 2023 CHI Conference on Human Factors in Computing Systems*, pages 1–14.

Ernie Chang, Xiaoyu Shen, Hui-Syuan Yeh, and Vera Demberg. 2021. On training instance selection for few-shot neural text generation. *arXiv preprint arXiv:2107.03176*.

Michael Desmond, Zahra Ashktorab, Qian Pan, Casey Dugan, and James M. Johnson. 2024. Evalullm: Llm assisted evaluation of generative outputs. In *Companion Proceedings of the 29th International Conference on Intelligent User Interfaces*, IUI '24 Companion, page 30–32, New York, NY, USA. Association for Computing Machinery.

Michael Desmond, Evelyn Duesterwald, Kristina Brimijoin, Michelle Brachman, and Qian Pan. 2021. Semi-automated data labeling. In *NeurIPS 2020 Competition and Demonstration Track*, pages 156–169. PMLR.

Markus Freitag, Ricardo Rei, Nitika Mathur, Chi-kiu Lo, Craig Stewart, Eleftherios Avramidis, Tom Kocmi, George Foster, Alon Lavie, and André FT Martins. 2022. Results of wmt22 metrics shared task: Stop using bleu–neural metrics are better and more robust. In *Proceedings of the Seventh Conference on Machine Translation (WMT)*, pages 46–68.

Jinlan Fu, See-Kiong Ng, Zhengbao Jiang, and Pengfei Liu. 2023. Gptscore: Evaluate as you desire. *arXiv preprint arXiv:2302.04166*.

Sebastian Gehrmann, Elizabeth Clark, and Thibault Sellam. 2023. Repairing the cracked foundation: A survey of obstacles in evaluation practices for generated text. *Journal of Artificial Intelligence Research*, 77:103–166.

Seungone Kim, Jamin Shin, Yejin Cho, Joel Jang, Shayne Longpre, Hwaran Lee, Sangdoo Yun, Seongjin Shin, Sungdong Kim, James Thorne, et al. 2023a. Prometheus: Inducing fine-grained evaluation capability in language models. *arXiv preprint arXiv:2310.08491*.

Tae Soo Kim, Yoonjoo Lee, Jamin Shin, Young-Ho Kim, and Juho Kim. 2023b. Evallm: Interactive evaluation of large language model prompts on user-defined criteria. *arXiv preprint arXiv:2309.13633*.

Tae Soo Kim, Yoonjoo Lee, Jamin Shin, Young-Ho Kim, and Juho Kim. 2023c. Evallm: Interactive evaluation of large language model prompts on user-defined criteria. In *arXiv preprint arXiv:2309.13633*.

Xuechen Li, Tianyi Zhang, Yann Dubois, Rohan Taori, Ishaan Gulrajani, Carlos Guestrin, Percy Liang, and Tatsunori B Hashimoto. 2023. Alpacaeval: An automatic evaluator of instruction-following models. *GitHub repository*.

Percy Liang, Rishi Bommasani, Tony Lee, Dimitris Tsipras, Dilara Soylu, Michihiro Yasunaga, Yian Zhang, Deepak Narayanan, Yuhuai Wu, Ananya Kumar, et al. 2022. Holistic evaluation of language models. *arXiv preprint arXiv:2211.09110*.

Chin-Yew Lin. 2004. Rouge: A package for automatic evaluation of summaries. In *Text summarization branches out*, pages 74–81.

Yang Liu, Dan Iter, Yichong Xu, Shuohang Wang, Ruochen Xu, and Chenguang Zhu. 2023a. Gpteval: Nlg evaluation using gpt-4 with better human alignment. *arXiv preprint arXiv:2303.16634*.

Yuxuan Liu, Tianchi Yang, Shaohan Huang, Zihan Zhang, Haizhen Huang, Furu Wei, Weiwei Deng, Feng Sun, and Qi Zhang. 2023b. Calibrating llm-based evaluator. *arXiv preprint arXiv:2309.13308*.

Kishore Papineni, Salim Roukos, Todd Ward, and Wei-Jing Zhu. 2002. Bleu: a method for automatic evaluation of machine translation. In *Proceedings of the 40th annual meeting of the Association for Computational Linguistics*, pages 311–318.

Savvas Petridis, Ben Wedin, James Wexler, Aaron Donsbach, Mahima Pushkarna, Nitesh Goyal, Carrie J Cai, and Michael Terry. 2023. Constitutionmaker: Interactively critiquing large language models by converting feedback into principles. *arXiv preprint arXiv:2310.15428*.

Keith E. Stanovich and Richard F. West. 2000. Advancing the rationality debate. *Behavioral and Brain Sciences*, 23(5):701–717.

Rickard Stureborg, Bhuwan Dhingra, and Jun Yang. 2023. Interface design for crowdsourcing hierarchical multi-label text annotations. In *Proceedings of the 2023 CHI Conference on Human Factors in Computing Systems*, pages 1–17.

Hongjin Su, Jungo Kasai, Chen Henry Wu, Weijia Shi, Tianlu Wang, Jiayi Xin, Rui Zhang, Mari Ostendorf, Luke Zettlemoyer, Noah A. Smith, and Tao Yu. 2022. Selective annotation makes language models better few-shot learners. *Preprint*, arXiv:2209.01975.

Jiaan Wang, Yunlong Liang, Fandong Meng, Haoxiang Shi, Zhixu Li, Jinan Xu, Jianfeng Qu, and Jie Zhou. 2023a. Is chatgpt a good nlg evaluator? a preliminary study. *arXiv preprint arXiv:2303.04048*.

Xuezhi Wang, Jason Wei, Dale Schuurmans, Quoc Le, Ed Chi, Sharan Narang, Aakanksha Chowdhery, and Denny Zhou. 2023b. Self-consistency improves chain of thought reasoning in language models. *Preprint*, arXiv:2203.11171.

Jason Wei, Xuezhi Wang, Dale Schuurmans, Maarten Bosma, Fei Xia, Ed Chi, Quoc V Le, Denny Zhou, et al. 2022. Chain-of-thought prompting elicits reasoning in large language models. *Advances in Neural Information Processing Systems*, 35:24824–24837.

James Wexler, Mahima Pushkarna, Tolga Bolukbasi, Martin Wattenberg, Fernanda Viégas, and Jimbo Wilson. 2019. The what-if tool: Interactive probing of machine learning models. *IEEE transactions on visualization and computer graphics*, 26(1):56–65.

Tongshuang Wu, Marco Tulio Ribeiro, Jeffrey Heer, and Daniel S Weld. 2019. Errudite: Scalable, reproducible, and testable error analysis. In *Proceedings of the 57th Annual Meeting of the Association for Computational Linguistics*, pages 747–763.

Ziang Xiao, Susu Zhang, Vivian Lai, and Q Vera Liao. 2023. Evaluating nlg evaluation metrics: A measurement theory perspective. *arXiv preprint arXiv:2305.14889*.

Weizhe Yuan, Richard Yuanzhe Pang, Kyunghyun Cho, Sainbayar Sukhbaatar, Jing Xu, and Jason Weston. 2024. Self-rewarding language models. *arXiv preprint arXiv:2401.10020*.

Lianmin Zheng, Wei-Lin Chiang, Ying Sheng, Siyuan Zhuang, Zhanghao Wu, Yonghao Zhuang, Zi Lin, Zhuohan Li, Dacheng Li, Eric Xing, et al. 2023. Judging llm-as-a-judge with mt-bench and chatbot arena. *arXiv preprint arXiv:2306.05685*.

A Participant Information

Table 1 shows the details of participants involved in the user study, predominantly comprising of industry experts such as data scientists, software engineers, and AI engineers. These professionals have practical experience in evaluating the performance of large language models in their projects over the last year.

B Summary of Evaluation Themes and Examples

Table 2 provides further details on evaluation themes generated from the user study, along with corresponding examples from participants' quotes.

C Recommended Designs

Figure (3)(4)(5) show design examples to help illustrate corresponding design recommendations.

D EvaluLLM Evaluation Workflow

Figure (6) shows the high-level overview of the EvaluLLM workflow, which consists of a Build, Review, and Inspect process.

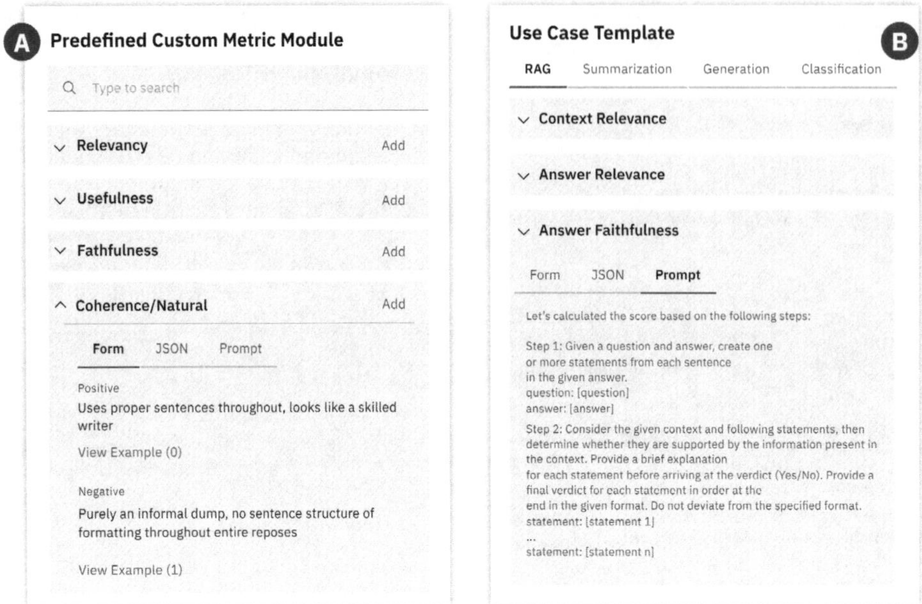

Figure 3: Recommended design to (A) enable users to choose from a list of predefined custom metric modules and (B) enable users to create a set of evaluation criteria based on common use cases.

ID	*Gender*	*Job Role*
P1	Male	Lead Software Engineer/Data Scientist
P2	Male	Principle Data Scientist
P3	Male	Lead Software Engineer/Data Scientist
P4	Male	Data Scientist
P5	Male	AI Engineer/Data Scientist
P6	Female	Data Scientist
P7	Male	Senior Technical Manager/Data Scientist
P8	Female	Data Scientist

Table 1: Demographic information from participants in our user study.

Table 2: Table of evaluation themes and corresponding examples. Themes are grouped into three categories: use case challenges, evaluation criteria, and evaluation workflow. Quotes are provided to delineate themes.

Group	**Theme**	**Example**
Use Case Challenges	Absence of Specifications	*"So we can compare using, metrics such as or BLEU, And this is like this other scenario, which unfortunately is more common, which is client doesn't even know what they want."* - P5 *"It was like eighty-twenty, eighty percent of the time they don't have it."* - P5
	Support Comparison with Different Setup	*"Say we had five different models and for each model we had 20 different configurations or something like that. Now that's 100 different combinations. Um, we'd like the limited judge to be to run on like all hundred. Give us an overview. Which are the three that are actually worth looking at?"* - P2 *"GPT 4 as a baseline and we're just trying to see how close are we getting with these other models in order to replicate the performance."* - P7
	Shifting Evaluation Priority	*"I know that's like a terrible metric [confusion matrix] to be used as the first one, but we have actually done this with a client because they asked us to do so. They're looking for just accuracy."* - P5 *"GPT 4 as a baseline and we're just trying to see how close are we getting with these other models in order to replicate the performance."* - P7
Evaluation Criteria	Desire Structured and Customizable Templates	*"A freeform text box is too simple. I would love there to be templates that I can utilize. And at the very least, be able to just edit so that I can get into my use case."* - P7 *"More examples might be nice."* - P2
	Need for Multiple Rounds of Iterations	*"It can be really hard to figure out how to express the evaluation criteria in a way that makes sense to the model. But it can also just be hard in your own mind to figure out what it means for a title to be good."* - P2 *"If I think, without having a clearer sense of what the evaluation is, sort of what a baseline evaluation is, it might be nice to have a couple of features of an evaluation that we could just select in like a checkbox. "* - P3
	Display Performance for each Criteria Individually	*"There might be times where you have to trade off on certain kinds of things and Win rate is not necessarily the best metric because there are multiple categories to define what it means to win."* - P7 *"So I'm covering a lot of ground there, and I know that's hard for the model to deal with because now the model has to have a whole lot of different criteria, and it's all drawn up by the ones, but that's kind of what a good title headline is about."* - P7
Evaluation Workflow	Run Evaluation on Subset of Data First	*"We don't have a problem here because the data set is small. But, like, if there's like, a 1000. Then it would it make sense to go through the entire batch and we find out your volume criteria needs to be tweaked."* - P2 *"I'd want to iterate on my judge enough for it to get a decent annotator agreement and then let it go wild."* - P2
	Instant Feedback on Human-AI agreement	*"Tell me when to quit."* -P1
	Ensuring Transparency for Trustworthy Evaluation	*"So I definitely want, as we discussed earlier, a lot of transparency and exactly what is being sent to the models to generate the responses and then what is then being sent to the LLM as a judge."* - P2 *"Maybe a small note on, like, you know what the prompt is, like, what the data set is and what the tool is doing."* - P8

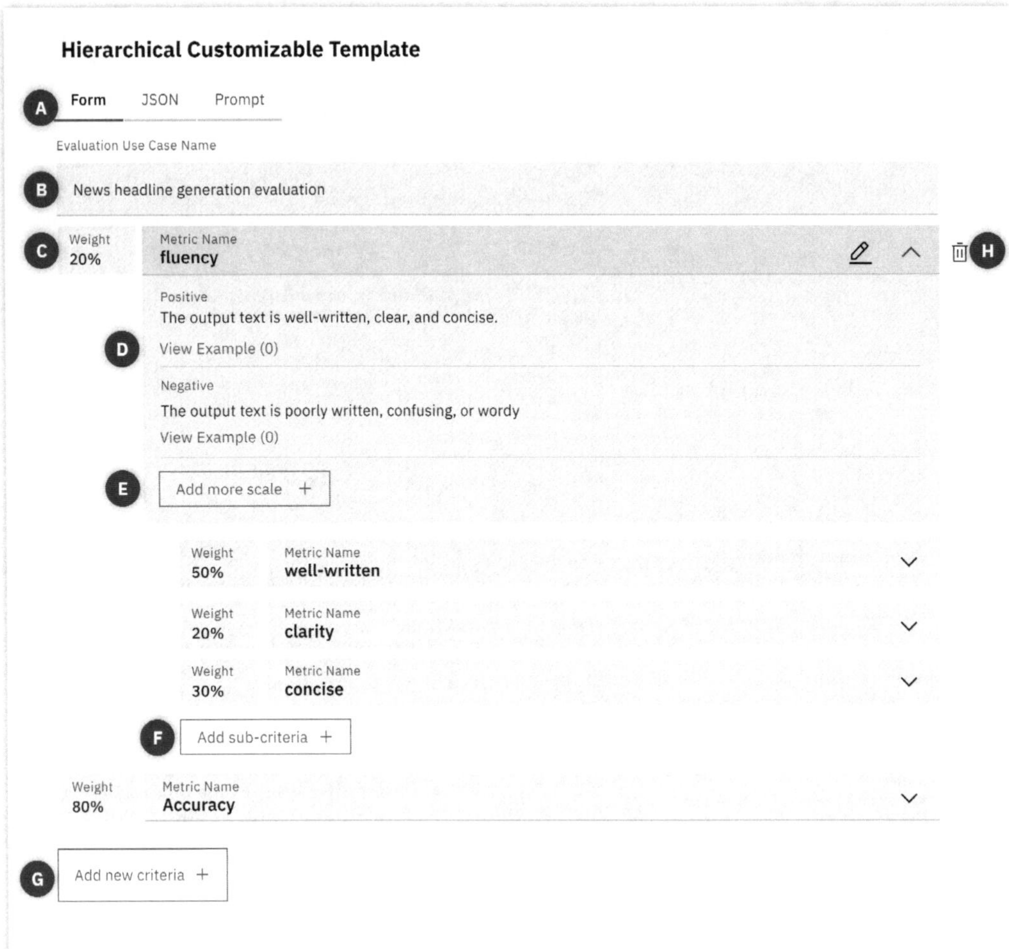

Figure 4: Recommended design to provide structured and customizable templates that support hierarchical, multi-dimensional evaluations.

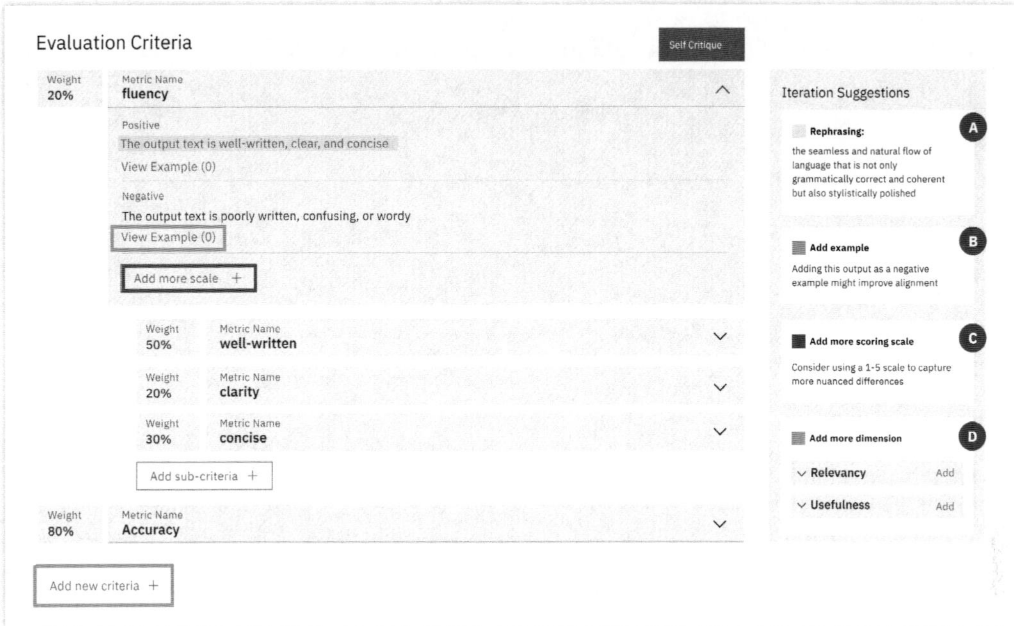

Figure 5: Recommended design demonstrating the ability of users to leverage LLM-as-a-Judge for Criteria Iteration.

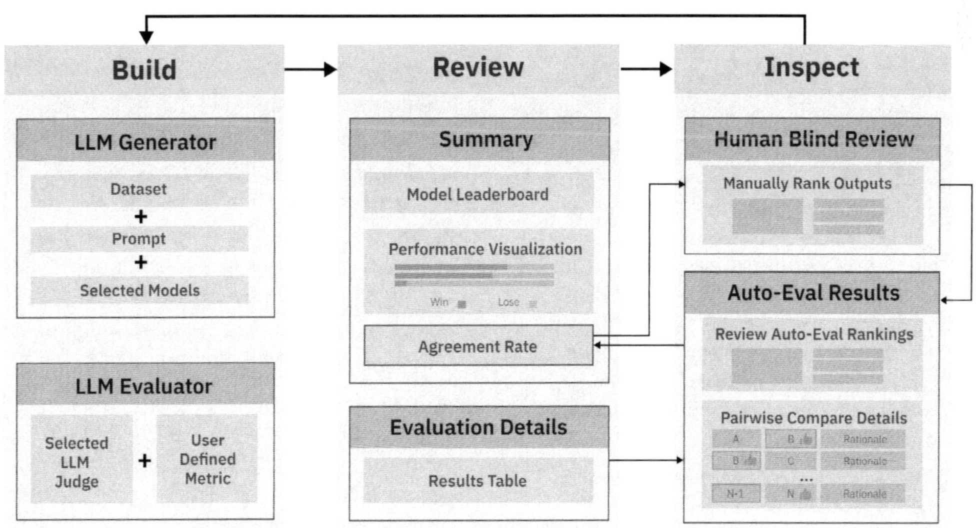

Figure 6: EvaluLLM evaluation workflow overview which consists of a Build, Review, and Inspect process.

Parameter-Efficient Detoxification with Contrastive Decoding

Tong Niu, Caiming Xiong, Yingbo Zhou*, Semih Yavuz*

Salesforce AI Research

Abstract

The field of natural language generation has witnessed significant advancements in recent years, including the development of controllable text generation techniques. However, controlling the attributes of the generated text remains a challenge, especially when aiming to avoid undesirable behavior such as toxicity. In this work, we introduce *Detoxification Generator* (DETOXIGEN), an inference-time algorithm that steers the generation away from unwanted styles. DETOXIGEN is an ensemble of a pre-trained language model (*generator*) and a *detoxifier*. The *detoxifier* is trained intentionally on the toxic data representative of the undesirable attribute, encouraging it to generate text in that style exclusively. During the actual generation, we use the trained *detoxifier* to produce undesirable tokens for the *generator* to contrast against at each decoding step. This approach directly informs the *generator* to avoid generating tokens that the *detoxifier* considers highly likely. We evaluate DETOXIGEN on the commonly used REALTOXICITYPROMPTS benchmark (Gehman et al., 2020) with various language models as *generators*. We find that it significantly outperforms previous approaches in detoxification metrics while not compromising on the generation quality. Moreover, the *detoxifier* is obtained by soft prompt-tuning using the same backbone language model as the *generator*. Hence, DETOXIGEN requires only a tiny amount of extra weights from the virtual tokens of the *detoxifier* to be loaded into GPU memory while decoding, making it a promising lightweight, practical, and parameter-efficient detoxification strategy.

1 Introduction

Large language models (LLMs) have demonstrated remarkable promise in various generative tasks by first self-supervised pretraining on large text corpora and then finetuning with instruction data for alignment (Mishra et al., 2022). Yet a wealth of previous work has demonstrated that pre-trained models inherit toxicity and biases from their training corpora (Zhao et al., 2019; May et al., 2019; Kurita et al., 2019; Basta et al., 2019). As a result, generative models (OpenAI, 2023; Touvron et al., 2023; Nijkamp et al., 2023) tend to degenerate into unsafe text even when conditioning on seemingly innocuous prompts (Wallace et al., 2019; Sheng et al., 2019; Gehman et al., 2020), which is difficult to resolve by prompt engineering alone (Zong and Krishnamachari, 2022; Liu et al., 2022b; Webson and Pavlick, 2022; Lou et al., 2023).

To address this challenge, a plethora of approaches have been proposed, which usually require full-model finetuning of the underlying language model to build the *detoxifier* (Dathathri et al., 2019; Gururangan et al., 2020; Krause et al., 2021; Liu et al., 2021a). However, nowadays the largest LLMs typically contain more than 100 billion parameters, making such resource-intensive tuning less viable. This trend calls for more parameter-efficient approaches.

In this work, we propose DETOXIGEN (Figure 1), a parameter-efficient framework that leverages the frozen weights of the language model itself and only introduces a tiny portion of new model parameters to detoxify generation.[1] During training, we use prompt tuning (Lester et al., 2021) to train a *detoxifier* exclusively on toxic data with the next-token prediction objective. The resulting *detoxifier* shares all the backbone model weights with the LLM (i.e., the *generator*). During inference, we build on top of the contrastive decoding (Li et al., 2023) paradigm and employ the *detoxifier* to manipulate the output probability distribution of the LLM for each generation step. Intuitively, the *generator* avoids outputting tokens that the *detoxifier* considers highly probable. For example, in figure 1 the

* indicates corresponding authors.

[1]We will make our code publicly available.

Proceedings of the 1st Human-Centered Large Language Modeling Workshop, pages 30–40
August 15, 2024

detoxifier considers the gender-biased word "his" very likely as the next token, helping the *generator* to score down the probability of that token.

We evaluate our framework on the REALTOXICITYPROMPTS dataset (Gehman et al., 2020) and find that it outperforms previous approaches on the standard benchmark metrics by a significant margin, indicating that the text generated by our model is both safer and of higher quality. We also conduct ablation studies and pair models of different sizes from the same model family (e.g., the Llama-2 (Touvron et al., 2023) family). These studies show that pairing a *generator* with a *detoxifier* that shares the same backbone LLM is indeed the best-performing configuration.

Our main contributions are: (1) Performance: Propose a detoxification framework that outperforms previous models by a large margin on commonly used detoxification benchmarks/metrics; (2) Efficiency: We apply parameter-efficient learning to controllable text generation for detoxification. Our model introduces the least amount of additional parameters (hence also requires less data to train) as compared to state-of-the-art models; (3) Transferability: Our *detoxifier* model only requires toxic data and does not require any contrastive (non-toxic) data, making our approach transferable thanks to the easier and more manageable data curation.

2 Model

2.1 Task Formulation

We consider controlled decoding-time approaches for open-ended text generation. A *generator*, in our case a language model, receives an unfinished input text as a prompt and aims to output a fluent and coherent continuation that avoids toxicity with the help of a *detoxifier*, which is another language model trained with data of the target attribute.

2.2 Model Components

Generator Let $x_{<t} = x_1, x_2, ..., x_{t-1}$ be a prompt consisting of $(t-1)$ tokens, where each $t_i (1 \leq i \leq t-1)$ is a token in the vocabulary set V of the language model (LM). The LM encodes $x_{<t}$ in an autoregressive fashion and outputs $\mathbf{z}_t \in \mathbb{R}^{|V|}$, where $\mathbf{z}_t$ denotes the logits for the tth token x_t and $|V|$ corresponds to the vocabulary size. The LM then obtains a probability distribution P_{GEN} over V by computing the softmax of $\mathbf{z}_t$

$$P_{GEN}(x_t|x_{<t}) = \text{softmax}(\mathbf{z}_t), \quad (1)$$

and the next token is sampled from this distribution.

Detoxifier The *detoxifier* takes as input the same prompt fed to the *generator* for each generation step and computes a probability distribution $P_{DE}(X_t|x_{<t})$ over $|V|$ in the same way. However, the *detoxifier* is not a vanilla LM like the *generator*, but rather an LM specially trained to output toxic content. Intuitively, the *generator* is discouraged from outputting tokens that the *detoxifier* considers highly likely, thus avoiding toxic generations. In other words, the decoding process involves an ensemble of the two LMs to obtain the final output probability distribution $P(x_t|x_{<t})$:

$$P(x_t|x_{<t}) = P_{GEN} + \alpha \Delta P \quad (2)$$

$$\Delta P = P_{GEN} - P_{DE}, \quad (3)$$

where the hyperparameter α denotes the *control strength* of the model and ΔP represents the *probability correction term* determined by the difference between the two distributions. Intuitively, α dictates how much we want to modify the *generator*'s probability distribution through the correction term ΔP. Since it is possible that $P(x_t|x_{<t})$ contains values that fall out of the $[0.0, 1.0]$ range, making them invalid probabilities, we also clip them on both sides – i.e., setting any value that is below 0.0 to 0.0 and any value above 1.0 to 1.0. The resulting probability vector is then normalized by first computing its log probabilities and then taking the softmax. Our formulation is closely related to that in Contrastive Decoding (Li et al., 2023) and DExperts (Liu et al., 2021a), but we differ by manipulating in the probability space rather than the logits space because we found in our initial experiments that directly dealing with probability distributions result in better performance on the downstream task.

Sampling To constrain the model to only generate plausible tokens, we first employ Nucleus (Top-p) Sampling (Holtzman et al., 2020) to limit the vocabulary V to a subset $V^{(p)}$ by only selecting the highest probability tokens whose cumulative probability mass exceeds some threshold $p \in [0.0, 1.0]$. More specifically, given the distribution $P_{GEN}(x_t|x_{<t})$ in Equation 1, the top-p

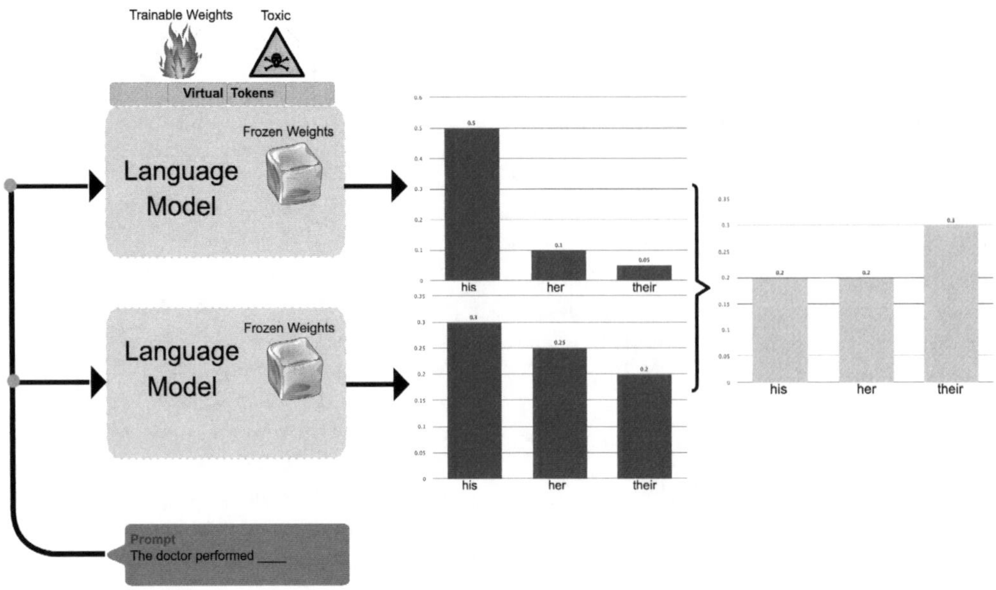

Figure 1: Illustration of the DETOXIGEN pipeline that avoids generating a gender-biased next token. A prompt is fed into both the *generator* and the *detoxifier*, which share the same underlying frozen weights from the backbone language model. Additionally, the *detoxifier* contains virtual tokens whose embeddings are trainable. Such virtual tokens steer the *detoxifier* toward generating only toxic continuations. Each model provides its own probability distribution for the next token, where DETOXIGEN combines the two distributions and performs the detoxification.

vocabulary $V^{(p)} \subseteq V$ is defined by the smallest vocabulary set such that

$$\sum_{x \in V^{(p)}} P_{GEN}(x|x_{<t}) \geq p. \tag{4}$$

The Top-p sampling then truncates the less reliable tail of the distribution by setting

$$P'[x] = \begin{cases} P[x], & \text{if } x \in V^{(p)} \\ 0, & \text{otherwise.} \end{cases} \tag{5}$$

The *detoxifier* then comes in and only manipulates logits in the set $V^{(p)}$ so that regardless of how P_{GEN} is modified, the generated tokens are guaranteed to be plausible as evaluated by the *generator*. When applying this restriction, equation 1 becomes

$$P'(x_t|x_{<t}) = P'_{GEN} + \alpha(P'_{GEN} - P'_{DE}). \tag{6}$$

2.3 Parameter-Efficient Training of Detoxifier

As discussed in Section 1, due to the increasing size of large language models, we aim to introduce as few additional model parameters as possible to our framework. Hence we adopt Prompt Tuning (Lester et al., 2021), a parameter-efficient training method, to train a language model exclusively on toxic data. This method learns soft prompts (or virtual tokens), whose embeddings are trainable parameters to condition frozen language models to perform the target downstream tasks.

3 Experimental Setup

3.1 Backbone Models

Following Liu et al. (2021a), we use GPT2-large (Radford et al., 2019) as the *generator* and the backbone of the *detoxifier*. We use GPT2-XL to evaluate the generation quality. For ablation studies reported in Section 4.3, we also consider GPT2 with small and medium sizes.

It is worth noting that previous work selected the GPT2 family mostly because it was one of the strongest models at the time. To observe if the same trend of performance holds for the most recent LLMs, we also experiment with another family of Transformer-based (Vaswani et al., 2017) language models, namely Llama-2 (Touvron et al., 2023) because it satisfies the following three criteria: (1) It is publicly released so that it is easier for researchers to reproduce and compare with our work; (2) It achieves state-of-the-art performance on diverse benchmark datasets (Nijkamp et al., 2023); (3) It has three sizes so that we can evaluate whether larger models can be paired with smaller ones for detoxification – such is the setting when we prioritize reducing latency over minimizing GPU memory footprint. Hence we experiment with Llama-2 with 7B, 13B, and 70B parameters, respectively. Due to the large size of Llama-2-70B, for all our experiments we use bfloat16 for both training and inference to increase throughput and reduce GPU memory usage. We evaluate perplexity from the Llama-2 family with Llama-2-7B unless otherwise stated.

3.2 Training of Detoxifier

We prompt tune the *detoxifier* with the standard language modeling objective (Bengio et al., 2000) which learns the parameters of the conditional probability distribution of the next word given the preceding context. We extract the training data from the human-annotated Jigsaw Unintended Bias in Toxicity Classification (Borkan et al., 2019). An example is considered toxic if more than 50% of the annotators classify it as toxic. This threshold splits the corpus into around 160K toxic and $1.4M$ nontoxic examples. We only train our models with the toxic part of the data.

For prompt tuning, we use 100 virtual tokens for each model with a learning rate of 0.1. To efficiently explore different parameter-efficient methods, we use the PEFT (Parameter-Efficient Fine-Tuning), a library that wraps around Hugging-Face Transformers (Wolf et al., 2020) model objects and provides out-of-the-box implementations for widely adopted PEFT approaches (Mangrulkar et al., 2022). Because we need to obtain logits from the *detoxifier* for each generation step, we overwrite the PEFT model object to only prepend virtual tokens to the input for the first generation step.

3.3 Hyperparameter Tuning

We tune the hyperparameter α with a held-out validation set and perform a grid search from 1.0 to 9.0 with a 1.0 increment. As will be shown in Section 4.1, we find that $\alpha = 5.0$ strikes the best balance between toxicity and generation quality. We thus adopt this value throughout all experiments.

3.4 Evaluation Data

We follow Liu et al. (2021a) to use the REALTOXICITYPROMPTS dataset (Gehman et al., 2020) which contains 100K naturally occurring, sentence-level prompts derived from a large corpus of English web text. These prompts are annotated with toxicity scores and language models are known to degenerate into toxic continuation when conditioning on them. To determine the *detoxifier* strength α, we randomly sample 1k prompts as the validation set and another disjoint 10k as the test set.

3.5 Metrics

Toxicity Following Gehman et al. (2020), we use the Perspective API[2] to measure the toxicity of generations. This score is obtained from a CNN model (Lecun et al., 1998) trained on a non-public corpus of Wikipedia comments. We compute two metrics based on the toxicity scores following Liu et al. (2021a): (1) Average Maximum Toxicity: The average maximum toxicity over $k = 25$ generations; (2) Toxicity Probability: The empirical probability of a generation with toxicity ≥ 0.5 for at least once over $k = 25$ generations.

Quality The Quality metric consists of both fluency and diversity. Heeding both aspects makes it easier to spot cases where the generation is likely but generic, or diverse but unlikely. We use corpus-level Perplexity to evaluate fluency and Distinct-2 and -3 (Li et al., 2016) to evaluate diversity. Distinct-2 and distinct-3 correspond respectively to the number of distinct bigrams and trigrams divided by the total number of generated words.

3.6 Baseline Models

We compare DETOXIGEN with a diverse set of previously reported baseline models (Gehman et al., 2020; Liu et al., 2021a), including Domain-Adaptive Pretraining (DAPT) (Gururangan et al., 2020), Plug-and-Play Language Models (PPLM) (Dathathri et al., 2019), Non-Toxic Expert (Liu et al., 2021a), Generative Discriminators (GeDi) (Krause et al., 2021), and Decoding-time Experts (DExperts) (Liu et al., 2021a). We follow these baselines to use Nucleus Sampling with $p = 0.9$ for generation.

[2] https://perspectiveapi.com/

4 Results and Analysis

4.1 Hyperparameter Tuning through Validation Set

As mentioned in Section 3.3, we perform a grid search of α with values $1.0, 2.0, ..., 9.0$. We show the results on both GPT2-large and Llama-2-7b so that we can observe the trend on both early and more recent models. From Table 2, we can see that for both models, there is a steady increase in Perplexity (last column) as α grows, indicating a monotonic decrease in generation quality. Intuitively, this trend makes sense because the more we perturb the original output distribution, the more likely it is for the language model to generate less plausible tokens. To maintain a balance between toxicity and quality, we seek the tipping point where further increasing α only brings a diminishing return on reducing toxicity. We observe that for both models, this tipping point happens at $\alpha = 5.0$. Hence we adopt this hyperparameter setting throughout all other experiments.

4.2 Results on GPT2-large

We then compare with previous approaches on GPT2-large. From Table 1, we can see that our model DETOXIGEN outperforms previous frameworks by a large margin although only tuned on the toxic split of the training data. Among all models, DETOXIGEN (GPT2-large) achieves the lowest Average Maximum Toxicity and Toxicity Probability, while obtaining a Perplexity that is quite close to that of the vanilla GPT-2 large, indicating minimum compromise on generation quality. The Llama-2-7B version of DETOXIGEN achieves even better results. However, it is based on a much stronger backbone language model, hence not comparable to previous work. We still include Llama-2 results in this table to show the gap between earlier and more recent large language models. We also follow Liu et al. (2021a) and report Distinct-N metrics, which are intended to prevent the model from degenerating into dull and generic continuations. We observe that the Distinct-N results do not vary much across diverse kinds of models. Hence for the results reported afterwards, we skip this metric and only report Perplexity.

4.3 Ablation Studies on Model Sizes

We also explore pairing models of different sizes as the *generator* and the *detoxifier*, respectively. This setting targets the cases where either latency is the major concern such that we want one small *detoxifier* to steer the generation of all other model sizes, or when we intend to train a *detoxifier* once and plug-and-play it with all other model sizes. The results of such pairings are presented in the matrix-like tables (Table 3, 5, 4, and 6). We report toxicity and quality in separate tables to make the comparisons clearer. From the four tables, we can observe quite a few interesting patterns.

Consistent Toxicity Reduction In the tables, we can observe that when comparing with the no-*detoxifier* setting (the column with *None* as header), our approach consistently and significantly reduces the toxicity of the backbone model while not sacrificing much on generation quality. This trend is observed for both the GPT-2 and the Llama-2 model families.

Entries along the Diagonal As shown in Table 3 and 4, entries on the diagonal of the result matrix (i.e., without the first column that has *None* as the header) consistently outperform their neighbors in terms of toxicity. These are the settings where the *generator* and the *detoxifier* share exactly the same backbone language model. They also achieve the best row-wise Perplexity as compared to off-diagonal models (Table 5 and 6). We hypothesize that this is because the output probability distributions of the *generator* and the *detoxifier* with the same underlying backbone parameters are more compatible with each other than backbones of different sizes. Recall in Section 1 that one of our major goals is to introduce as few new model parameters as possible. Our cross-model results clearly show that sharing weights between the *generator* and the *detoxifier* turns out to be the best setting among all we have investigated.

Entries symmetric to the diagonal Comparing entries that are symmetric to the diagonal (e.g., comparing GPT2-XL detoxified by GPT2-small with GPT2-small detoxified by GPT2-XL) in Table 3 and 4, we can observe a consistent pattern that given two models of different sizes, it is usually better to have the smaller model as the *generator* and the larger model as the *detoxifier* for detoxification. This indicates that larger models are more capable of capturing the distribution in the toxicity training corpus.

Effect of Model Size Difference From the toxicity tables, we can also observe that the larger the

Table 1: Results on a random nontoxic 10K sample from the REALTOXICITYPROMPTS dataset. On the first row, the downward arrows indicate "the lower the better", while the upward ones indicate the opposite. Avg. Max. Toxicity stands for "Average Maximum Toxicity", PPL stands for "Perplexity", and all models are evaluated with GPT2-XL. Dist-N stands for the Distinct-N metric. All models in this table use GPT2-large as the backbone model, except for the last row where Llama-2-7B is used. State-of-the-art results are boldfaced.

Model	**Toxicity** (↓)		**Fluency** (↓)	**Diversity** (↑)	
	Avg. Max. Toxicity	Toxicity Prob.	PPL	Dist-2	Dist-3
GPT2-large	0.527	0.520	25.45	0.85	0.85
PPLM	0.520	0.518	32.58	**0.86**	0.86
Non-toxic Expert	0.485	0.464	40.61	**0.86**	0.86
DAPT	0.428	0.360	31.21	0.84	0.84
GeDi	0.363	0.217	60.03	0.84	0.83
DExperts	0.314	0.128	32.41	0.84	0.84
DETOXIGEN (GPT2-large)	**0.254**	**0.115**	**27.54**	**0.86**	**0.86**
DETOXIGEN (Llama-2-7B)	**0.236**	**0.103**	**26.55**	0.85	0.84

Table 2: Validation results obtained by varying the *detoxifier* strength α from 1.0 to 9.0 with GPT2-large and Llama-2-7b. Each setting is evaluated on a held-out validation set of size 1k from REALTOXICITYPROMPTS. The boldfaced rows indicate tipping points where further increasing α starts to bring diminishing (sometimes even negative) returns on the balance between toxicity and fluency.

Model	**Alpha**	**Toxicity** (↓)		**Fluency** (↓)
		Avg. Max. Toxicity	Toxicity Prob.	PPL
	1.0	0.311	0.172	22.47
	2.0	0.284	0.145	23.54
	3.0	0.276	0.146	24.66
	4.0	0.261	0.127	25.83
GPT2-large	**5.0**	**0.258**	**0.115**	**26.65**
	6.0	0.261	0.128	27.54
	7.0	0.256	0.121	28.19
	8.0	0.257	0.125	28.82
	9.0	0.258	0.108	29.59
	1.0	0.290	0.160	19.88
	2.0	0.265	0.127	20.61
	3.0	0.252	0.108	21.20
	4.0	0.251	0.117	21.74
Llama-2-7b	**5.0**	**0.241**	**0.104**	**22.31**
	6.0	0.243	0.101	22.79
	7.0	0.241	0.106	23.13
	8.0	0.236	0.094	23.51
	9.0	0.233	0.097	23.88

model size difference, the less effective the detoxification. For example, GPT2-XL detoxified by GPT2-small in Table 3 results in the worst toxicity among all settings, while we observe the same pattern where Llama-2-70B detoxified by Llama-2-7B has the highest toxicity among all settings.

5 Discussion

It would be ideal if a *detoxifier* could work out of the box (plug-and-play) and be readily applied to any LLM *generator*, even with a different tokenizer. To achieve this, one can take a common subset of the vocabulary sets between the *generator* and the *detoxifier*, and only manipulate logits on this subset. We leave this as future work since the model families we investigate both already have diverse sizes.

Throughout the paper, we have been focusing on avoiding undesired attributes. However, we note that our framework can also be used to generate text with any desired style (which could be a risk if that desire style happens to be *toxic*). All we need to do is flip the sign of the probability distribution correction term ΔP in Equation 2 and 3 as follows:

$$P(x_t|x_{<t}) = P_{GEN} + \alpha\Delta P \tag{7}$$

$$\Delta P = P_{DE} - P_{GEN}. \tag{8}$$

In addition, our approach could be applied to more general positive and negative attributes, including but not limited to politeness (Danescu-Niculescu-Mizil et al., 2013; Niu and Bansal, 2018), hate speech (Golbeck et al., 2017), and microagressions (Breitfeller et al., 2019). In the case

Table 3: Toxicity results by pairing models of different sizes from the GPT-2 model family. All results are obtained on the validation set of size 1K. The column with the header *None* indicates that no *detoxifier* is used.

		detoxifier [Avg. Max. Toxicity | Toxicity Prob.]				
		None	GPT2-small	GPT2-medium	GPT2-large	GPT2-XL
generator	GPT2-small	0.511 | 0.413	0.264 | 0.119	0.306 | 0.161	0.318 | 0.183	0.330 | 0.195
	GPT2-medium	0.514 | 0.413	0.338 | 0.195	0.280 | 0.149	0.313 | 0.182	0.331 | 0.201
	GPT2-large	0.499 | 0.400	0.340 | 0.215	0.322 | 0.197	0.254| 0.115	0.314 | 0.175
	GPT2-XL	0.508 | 0.432	0.352 | 0.230	0.339 | 0.202	0.313 | 0.177	0.278 | 0.124

Table 4: Toxicity results by pairing models of different sizes from the Llama-2 model family. All results are obtained on the validation set of size 1K. The column with the header *None* indicates that no *detoxifier* is used.

		detoxifier [Avg. Max. Toxicity | Toxicity Prob.]			
		None	LLama-2-7B	LLama-2-13B	LLama-2-70B
generator	LLama-2-7B	0.370 | 0.285	0.241 | 0.104	0.268 | 0.131	0.287 | 0.155
	LLama-2-13B	0.371 | 0.275	0.285 | 0.143	0.248 | 0.112	0.295 | 0.164
	LLama-2-70B	0.371 | 0.276	0.295 | 0.157	0.293 | 0.167	0.277 | 0.157

that we want to simultaneously control for multiple attributes, our framework is also compatible with mixed-batch inference (Liu et al., 2022a), where soft prompts of different attributes can be conditioned on in a single batch without increasing latency.

6 Related Work

6.1 Parameter-efficient Learning

Parameter-efficient learning is a natural language processing paradigm to adapt a large language model to particular tasks or domains. It is usually used when fine-tuning the entire language model is prohibitively expensive. Among such approaches, LoRa (Hu et al., 2022) and AdaLoRa (Zhang et al., 2023) inject trainable rank decomposition matrices into each layer of the Transformer architecture, with the latter adaptively allocating the parameter budget among weight matrices according to their importance scores. Prefix Tuning (Li and Liang, 2021), P-Tuning (Liu et al., 2021b), and Prompt Tuning (Lester et al., 2021) prepend to the input sequence virtual tokens with trainable embeddings. Lastly, $(IA)^3$ scales activations by learned vectors. We choose Prompt Tuning in this work because it achieves competitive performance while involving no change in model architecture and not requiring any bootstrapping for the newly introduced model parameters.

6.2 Controllable Text Generation

There have been multiple effective frameworks proposed for controllable text generation (Keskar et al., 2019; Sudhakar et al., 2019; Kurita et al., 2019; Welleck et al., 2020). [3] Among them, Domain-Adaptive Pretraining (DAPT) (Gururangan et al., 2020) and Self-Generation Enabled domain-Adaptive Training (SGEAT) (Wang et al., 2022) continues to finetune or apply parameter-efficient tuning to the backbone language model with a non-toxic subset of OpenWebText to adapt it to the non-toxic style. Plug-and-Play Language Models (PPLM) (Dathathri et al., 2019) trains a toxicity classifier and leverages gradients from that classifier to update the language model's hidden representations for each generation step. Generative Discriminators (GeDi) (Krause et al., 2021) prepends to the input a soft token serving as the label for the intended class of attribute. It can be viewed as prompt tuning with only one virtual token for each class (toxic and nontoxic). Decoding-time Experts (DExperts) (Liu et al., 2021a) train an expert and an anti-expert LM of opposing attributes with full finetuning. During inference, the logits difference between the two experts serves as the correction term for the logits of the base language model. Our work is different from the previous approaches in that we adopt parameter-efficient tuning that only introduces a few trainable parameters and our training only requires toxic examples rather than examples from both classes.

6.3 Contrastive Decoding

Contrastive Decoding (Li et al., 2023; O'Brien and Lewis, 2023) is a search-based decoding method that optimizes a contrastive objective that returns

[3] We note that Inference-Time Policy Adapters (Lu et al., 2023) employs reinforcement learning for LM detoxification, but their approach assumes access to the Perspective API toxicity scores as a reward signal during training and hence not comparable to our work.

Table 5: Quality results by pairing models of different sizes from the GPT-2 model family. All results are obtained on the validation set of size 1K. The column with the header *None* indicates that no *detoxifier* is used.

		detoxifier [PPL]				
		None	GPT2-small	GPT2-medium	GPT2-large	GPT2-XL
generator	GPT2-small	49.90	60.46	76.83	82.90	91.02
	GPT2-medium	36.91	38.38	39.73	51.00	58.64
	GPT2-large	25.05	25.77	27.57	27.54	37.08
	GPT2-XL	18.16	18.54	18.76	19.77	19.80

Table 6: Quality results by pairing models of different sizes from the Llama-2 model family. All results are obtained on the validation set of size 1K. The column with the header *None* indicates that no *detoxifier* is used.

		detoxifier [PPL]			
		None	LLama-2-7B	LLama-2-13B	LLama-2-70B
generator	LLama-2-7B	19.65	22.94	23.12	22.35
	LLama-2-13B	21.69	28.38	25.47	26.90
	LLama-2-70B	22.39	29.68	28.68	26.55

the difference between the likelihood under a large and a small LM. Our algorithm is different from theirs in that we pair LMs of the same size (with the *detoxifier* further tuned) and perform all manipulations in the probability space rather than directly in the logits space.

7 Conclusion

We propose DETOXIGEN, a high-performing, parameter-efficient framework for detoxification during inference time. Our method only introduces a small portion of new parameters to train a *detoxifier* model that manipulates the output probability distribution of a generative model. On a standard detoxification benchmark, our approach outperforms all existing models in terms of both toxicity and quality. As language models grow ever larger in size, our controllable generation method shows the promise of quickly adapting to any language model without requiring additional computational resources or significant data curation efforts.

8 Limitations

Although DETOXIGEN can work with models of different sizes, it is yet to show that a *generator* with tokenizer A can be paired with a *detoxifier* that uses tokenizer B with a different vocabulary set. We plan to address this limitation in future work where the *detoxifier* can tokenize the generated text on the fly for each generation step, thus manipulating the logits of the *generator*. Additionally, although leveraging the Perspective API makes our model readily comparable with previous work, such automatic evaluation may not capture the full spectrum of toxicity. Ideally, one would conduct human evaluations for each of the models under the same setting. Lastly, it would be helpful to show how our method generalizes to other styles and parameter-efficient tuning approaches.

References

Christine Basta, Marta R. Costa-jussà, and Noe Casas. 2019. Evaluating the underlying gender bias in contextualized word embeddings. In *Proceedings of the First Workshop on Gender Bias in Natural Language Processing*, pages 33–39, Florence, Italy. Association for Computational Linguistics.

Yoshua Bengio, Réjean Ducharme, and Pascal Vincent. 2000. A neural probabilistic language model. *Advances in neural information processing systems*, 13.

Daniel Borkan, Jeffrey Sorensen, Lucas Dixon, and Lucy Vasserman. 2019. Jigsaw unintended bias in toxicity classification.

Luke Breitfeller, Emily Ahn, David Jurgens, and Yulia Tsvetkov. 2019. Finding microaggressions in the wild: A case for locating elusive phenomena in social media posts. In *Proceedings of the 2019 Conference on Empirical Methods in Natural Language Processing and the 9th International Joint Conference on Natural Language Processing (EMNLP-IJCNLP)*, pages 1664–1674, Hong Kong, China. Association for Computational Linguistics.

Cristian Danescu-Niculescu-Mizil, Moritz Sudhof, Dan Jurafsky, Jure Leskovec, and Christopher Potts. 2013. A computational approach to politeness with application to social factors. In *Proceedings of the 51st Annual Meeting of the Association for Computational Linguistics (Volume 1: Long Papers)*, pages 250–259, Sofia, Bulgaria. Association for Computational Linguistics.

Sumanth Dathathri, Andrea Madotto, Janice Lan, Jane Hung, Eric Frank, Piero Molino, Jason Yosinski, and

Rosanne Liu. 2019. Plug and play language models: A simple approach to controlled text generation. *arXiv preprint arXiv:1912.02164*.

Samuel Gehman, Suchin Gururangan, Maarten Sap, Yejin Choi, and Noah A. Smith. 2020. RealToxicityPrompts: Evaluating neural toxic degeneration in language models. In *Findings of the Association for Computational Linguistics: EMNLP 2020*, pages 3356–3369, Online. Association for Computational Linguistics.

Jennifer Golbeck, Zahra Ashktorab, Rashad O. Banjo, Alexandra Berlinger, Siddharth Bhagwan, Cody Buntain, Paul Cheakalos, Alicia A. Geller, Quint Gergory, Rajesh Kumar Gnanasekaran, Raja Rajan Gunasekaran, Kelly M. Hoffman, Jenny Hottle, Vichita Jienjitlert, Shivika Khare, Ryan Lau, Marianna J. Martindale, Shalmali Naik, Heather L. Nixon, Piyush Ramachandran, Kristine M. Rogers, Lisa Rogers, Meghna Sardana Sarin, Gaurav Shahane, Jayanee Thanki, Priyanka Vengataraman, Zijian Wan, and Derek Michael Wu. 2017. A large labeled corpus for online harassment research. In *Proceedings of the 2017 ACM on Web Science Conference*, WebSci '17, page 229–233, New York, NY, USA. Association for Computing Machinery.

Suchin Gururangan, Ana Marasović, Swabha Swayamdipta, Kyle Lo, Iz Beltagy, Doug Downey, and Noah A. Smith. 2020. Don't stop pretraining: Adapt language models to domains and tasks. In *Proceedings of the 58th Annual Meeting of the Association for Computational Linguistics*, pages 8342–8360, Online. Association for Computational Linguistics.

Ari Holtzman, Jan Buys, Li Du, Maxwell Forbes, and Yejin Choi. 2020. The curious case of neural text degeneration. In *International Conference on Learning Representations*.

Edward J Hu, yelong shen, Phillip Wallis, Zeyuan Allen-Zhu, Yuanzhi Li, Shean Wang, Lu Wang, and Weizhu Chen. 2022. LoRA: Low-rank adaptation of large language models. In *International Conference on Learning Representations*.

Nitish Shirish Keskar, Bryan McCann, Lav R Varshney, Caiming Xiong, and Richard Socher. 2019. Ctrl: A conditional transformer language model for controllable generation. *arXiv preprint arXiv:1909.05858*.

Ben Krause, Akhilesh Deepak Gotmare, Bryan McCann, Nitish Shirish Keskar, Shafiq Joty, Richard Socher, and Nazneen Fatema Rajani. 2021. GeDi: Generative discriminator guided sequence generation. In *Findings of the Association for Computational Linguistics: EMNLP 2021*, pages 4929–4952, Punta Cana, Dominican Republic. Association for Computational Linguistics.

Keita Kurita, Nidhi Vyas, Ayush Pareek, Alan W Black, and Yulia Tsvetkov. 2019. Measuring bias in contextualized word representations. In *Proceedings of the First Workshop on Gender Bias in Natural Language Processing*, pages 166–172, Florence, Italy. Association for Computational Linguistics.

Y. Lecun, L. Bottou, Y. Bengio, and P. Haffner. 1998. Gradient-based learning applied to document recognition. *Proceedings of the IEEE*, 86(11):2278–2324.

Brian Lester, Rami Al-Rfou, and Noah Constant. 2021. The power of scale for parameter-efficient prompt tuning. In *Proceedings of the 2021 Conference on Empirical Methods in Natural Language Processing*, pages 3045–3059, Online and Punta Cana, Dominican Republic. Association for Computational Linguistics.

Jiwei Li, Michel Galley, Chris Brockett, Jianfeng Gao, and Bill Dolan. 2016. A diversity-promoting objective function for neural conversation models. In *Proceedings of the 2016 Conference of the North American Chapter of the Association for Computational Linguistics: Human Language Technologies*, pages 110–119, San Diego, California. Association for Computational Linguistics.

Xiang Lisa Li, Ari Holtzman, Daniel Fried, Percy Liang, Jason Eisner, Tatsunori Hashimoto, Luke Zettlemoyer, and Mike Lewis. 2023. Contrastive decoding: Open-ended text generation as optimization. In *Proceedings of the 61st Annual Meeting of the Association for Computational Linguistics (Volume 1: Long Papers)*, pages 12286–12312, Toronto, Canada. Association for Computational Linguistics.

Xiang Lisa Li and Percy Liang. 2021. Prefix-tuning: Optimizing continuous prompts for generation. In *Proceedings of the 59th Annual Meeting of the Association for Computational Linguistics and the 11th International Joint Conference on Natural Language Processing (Volume 1: Long Papers)*, pages 4582–4597, Online. Association for Computational Linguistics.

Alisa Liu, Maarten Sap, Ximing Lu, Swabha Swayamdipta, Chandra Bhagavatula, Noah A. Smith, and Yejin Choi. 2021a. DExperts: Decoding-time controlled text generation with experts and anti-experts. In *Proceedings of the 59th Annual Meeting of the Association for Computational Linguistics and the 11th International Joint Conference on Natural Language Processing (Volume 1: Long Papers)*, pages 6691–6706, Online. Association for Computational Linguistics.

Haokun Liu, Derek Tam, Muqeeth Mohammed, Jay Mohta, Tenghao Huang, Mohit Bansal, and Colin Raffel. 2022a. Few-shot parameter-efficient fine-tuning is better and cheaper than in-context learning. In *Advances in Neural Information Processing Systems*.

Tianyu Liu, Yizhe Zhang, Chris Brockett, Yi Mao, Zhifang Sui, Weizhu Chen, and Bill Dolan. 2022b. A token-level reference-free hallucination detection benchmark for free-form text generation. In *Proceedings of the 60th Annual Meeting of the Association for Computational Linguistics (Volume 1: Long Papers)*, pages 6723–6737, Dublin, Ireland. Association for Computational Linguistics.

X Liu, Y Zheng, Z Du, M Ding, Y Qian, Z Yang, and J Tang. 2021b. Gpt understands, too. arxiv. *arXiv preprint arXiv:2103.10385*.

Renze Lou, Kai Zhang, and Wenpeng Yin. 2023. Is prompt all you need? no. a comprehensive and broader view of instruction learning. *arXiv preprint arXiv:2303.10475*.

Ximing Lu, Faeze Brahman, Peter West, Jaehun Jang, Khyathi Chandu, Abhilasha Ravichander, Lianhui Qin, Prithviraj Ammanabrolu, Liwei Jiang, Sahana Ramnath, et al. 2023. Inference-time policy adapters (ipa): Tailoring extreme-scale lms without fine-tuning. *arXiv preprint arXiv:2305.15065*.

Sourab Mangrulkar, Sylvain Gugger, Lysandre Debut, Younes Belkada, and Sayak Paul. 2022. Peft: State-of-the-art parameter-efficient fine-tuning methods. `https://github.com/huggingface/peft`.

Chandler May, Alex Wang, Shikha Bordia, Samuel R. Bowman, and Rachel Rudinger. 2019. On measuring social biases in sentence encoders. In *Proceedings of the 2019 Conference of the North American Chapter of the Association for Computational Linguistics: Human Language Technologies, Volume 1 (Long and Short Papers)*, pages 622–628, Minneapolis, Minnesota. Association for Computational Linguistics.

Swaroop Mishra, Daniel Khashabi, Chitta Baral, and Hannaneh Hajishirzi. 2022. Cross-task generalization via natural language crowdsourcing instructions. In *Proceedings of the 60th Annual Meeting of the Association for Computational Linguistics (Volume 1: Long Papers)*, pages 3470–3487, Dublin, Ireland. Association for Computational Linguistics.

Erik Nijkamp, Tian Xie, Hiroaki Hayashi, Bo Pang, Congying Xia, Chen Xing, Jesse Vig, Semih Yavuz, Philippe Laban, Ben Krause, et al. 2023. Xgen-7b technical report. *arXiv preprint arXiv:2309.03450*.

Tong Niu and Mohit Bansal. 2018. Polite dialogue generation without parallel data. *Transactions of the Association for Computational Linguistics*, 6:373–389.

Sean O'Brien and Mike Lewis. 2023. Contrastive decoding improves reasoning in large language models. *arXiv preprint arXiv:2309.09117*.

OpenAI. 2023. Gpt-4 technical report.

Alec Radford, Jeffrey Wu, Rewon Child, David Luan, Dario Amodei, Ilya Sutskever, et al. 2019. Language models are unsupervised multitask learners. *OpenAI blog*, 1(8):9.

Emily Sheng, Kai-Wei Chang, Premkumar Natarajan, and Nanyun Peng. 2019. The woman worked as a babysitter: On biases in language generation. In *Proceedings of the 2019 Conference on Empirical Methods in Natural Language Processing and the 9th International Joint Conference on Natural Language Processing (EMNLP-IJCNLP)*, pages 3407–3412, Hong Kong, China. Association for Computational Linguistics.

Akhilesh Sudhakar, Bhargav Upadhyay, and Arjun Maheswaran. 2019. "transforming" delete, retrieve, generate approach for controlled text style transfer. In *Proceedings of the 2019 Conference on Empirical Methods in Natural Language Processing and the 9th International Joint Conference on Natural Language Processing (EMNLP-IJCNLP)*, pages 3269–3279, Hong Kong, China. Association for Computational Linguistics.

Hugo Touvron, Louis Martin, Kevin Stone, Peter Albert, Amjad Almahairi, Yasmine Babaei, Nikolay Bashlykov, Soumya Batra, Prajjwal Bhargava, Shruti Bhosale, et al. 2023. Llama 2: Open foundation and fine-tuned chat models. *arXiv preprint arXiv:2307.09288*.

Ashish Vaswani, Noam Shazeer, Niki Parmar, Jakob Uszkoreit, Llion Jones, Aidan N. Gomez, Łukasz Kaiser, and Illia Polosukhin. 2017. Attention is all you need. In *Proceedings of the 31st International Conference on Neural Information Processing Systems*, NIPS'17, page 6000–6010, Red Hook, NY, USA. Curran Associates Inc.

Eric Wallace, Shi Feng, Nikhil Kandpal, Matt Gardner, and Sameer Singh. 2019. Universal adversarial triggers for attacking and analyzing NLP. In *Proceedings of the 2019 Conference on Empirical Methods in Natural Language Processing and the 9th International Joint Conference on Natural Language Processing (EMNLP-IJCNLP)*, pages 2153–2162, Hong Kong, China. Association for Computational Linguistics.

Boxin Wang, Wei Ping, Chaowei Xiao, Peng Xu, Mostofa Patwary, Mohammad Shoeybi, Bo Li, Anima Anandkumar, and Bryan Catanzaro. 2022. Exploring the limits of domain-adaptive training for detoxifying large-scale language models. *Advances in Neural Information Processing Systems*, 35:35811–35824.

Albert Webson and Ellie Pavlick. 2022. Do prompt-based models really understand the meaning of their prompts? In *Proceedings of the 2022 Conference of the North American Chapter of the Association for Computational Linguistics: Human Language Technologies*, pages 2300–2344, Seattle, United States. Association for Computational Linguistics.

Sean Welleck, Ilia Kulikov, Stephen Roller, Emily Dinan, Kyunghyun Cho, and Jason Weston. 2020. Neural text generation with unlikelihood training. In *International Conference on Learning Representations*.

Thomas Wolf, Lysandre Debut, Victor Sanh, Julien Chaumond, Clement Delangue, Anthony Moi, Pierric Cistac, Tim Rault, Remi Louf, Morgan Funtowicz, Joe Davison, Sam Shleifer, Patrick von Platen, Clara Ma, Yacine Jernite, Julien Plu, Canwen Xu, Teven Le Scao, Sylvain Gugger, Mariama Drame, Quentin Lhoest, and Alexander Rush. 2020. Transformers: State-of-the-art natural language processing. In *Proceedings of the 2020 Conference on Empirical Methods in Natural Language Processing: System Demonstrations*, pages 38–45, Online. Association for Computational Linguistics.

Qingru Zhang, Minshuo Chen, Alexander Bukharin, Pengcheng He, Yu Cheng, Weizhu Chen, and Tuo Zhao. 2023. Adaptive budget allocation for parameter-efficient fine-tuning. In *The Eleventh International Conference on Learning Representations*.

Jieyu Zhao, Tianlu Wang, Mark Yatskar, Ryan Cotterell, Vicente Ordonez, and Kai-Wei Chang. 2019. Gender bias in contextualized word embeddings. In *Proceedings of the 2019 Conference of the North American Chapter of the Association for Computational Linguistics: Human Language Technologies, Volume 1 (Long and Short Papers)*, pages 629–634, Minneapolis, Minnesota. Association for Computational Linguistics.

Mingyu Zong and Bhaskar Krishnamachari. 2022. A survey on gpt-3. *arXiv preprint arXiv:2212.00857*.

To What Extent Are Large Language Models Capable of Generating Substantial Reflections for Motivational Interviewing Counseling Chatbots? A Human Evaluation

Erkan Başar[1], Iris Hendrickx[2], Emiel Krahmer[3], Gert-Jan de Bruijn[4], and Tibor Bosse[1]
[1]Behavioural Science Institute, Radboud University, The Netherlands
[2]Centre for Language Studies, Radboud University, The Netherlands
[3]Tilburg School of Humanities and Digital Sciences, Tilburg University, The Netherlands
[4]Department of Communication Studies, University of Antwerp, Belgium
{erkan.basar, iris.hendrickx, tibor.bosse}@ru.nl,
e.j.krahmer@tilburguniversity.edu, gert-jan.debruijn@uantwerpen.be

Abstract

Motivational Interviewing is a counselling style that requires skillful usage of reflective listening and engaging in conversations about sensitive and personal subjects. In this paper, we investigate to what extent we can use generative large language models in motivational interviewing chatbots to generate precise and variable reflections on user responses. We conduct a two-step human evaluation where we first independently assess the generated reflections based on four criteria essential to health counseling; appropriateness, specificity, naturalness, and engagement. In the second step, we compare the overall quality of generated and human-authored reflections via a ranking evaluation. We use GPT-4, BLOOM, and FLAN-T5 models to generate motivational interviewing reflections, based on real conversational data collected via chatbots designed to provide support for smoking cessation and sexual health. We discover that GPT-4 can produce reflections of a quality comparable to human-authored reflections. Finally, we conclude that large language models have the potential to enhance and expand reflections in predetermined health counseling chatbots, but a comprehensive manual review is advised.

1 Introduction

Motivational Interviewing (MI) is a counseling style for eliciting behavior change, where the counselors guide individuals towards evoking their intrinsic motivations by addressing and resolving their ambivalence (Miller and Rollnick, 2012). A crucial technique that MI counselors utilize is *reflective listening*, where they engage in attentive listening and offer reflections on their clients' perspectives. A *reflection* is a special form of utterance where the counselor deliberates on the client's statements and articulates it back, often emphasizing the emotional content or underlying meaning.

Health counseling via chatbots is a domain that demands high accuracy in personalization along careful and appropriate language usage. Typically, MI-based chatbots are designed to follow a predetermined set of dialogue steps to guide the counseling session through the required MI phases (He et al., 2022). The process of creating a prewritten collection of human-authored responses is laborious and the lack of limited flexibility often leads to the use of generalized reflections. The restricted number of reflections may result in vagueness and hinder the chatbot's ability to exhibit empathy. Automating the process of generating reflections has the potential to enhance the personalization, accuracy, and effectiveness of counseling chatbots.

Generative Large Language Models (LLMs) have advanced to a stage where the coherency and fluency of the generated text makes it increasingly challenging to distinguish it from human-authored text (Gao et al., 2023). However, the potential dangers associated with inflammatory language, hallucinations, and the underlying fundamental issues continue to exist (Bender et al., 2021; Ji et al., 2023). Engaging in MI counseling requires addressing highly sensitive subjects, and unfitting reflections can impede or even undermine patients' advancement toward their behavior change objectives (Miller and Rollnick, 2012). This necessitates careful consideration and thorough evaluation before determining the potential applicability of LLMs for reflection generation.

Previous studies with LLMs for the MI reflection generation has yielded positive outcomes across different evaluation criteria. Fine-tuning a GPT-2 (Radford et al., 2019) model has showcased its ability to generate reflections that evaluators consider to be similar in quality and reflection-likeness

Proceedings of the 1st Human-Centered Large Language Modeling Workshop, pages 41–52
August 15, 2024 ©2024 Association for Computational Linguistics

to the ground truth reflections (Shen et al., 2022). Likewise, a few-shots prompted GPT-3 (Brown et al., 2020) can generate reflections that human evaluators deem acceptable (Ahmed, 2022). Moreover, the more recent GPT-4 (OpenAI, 2023) with zero-shot prompting can generate reflections that human evaluators have classified as adhering to MI principles in 99% of the cases from human-chatbot conversations on smoking cessation (Brown et al., 2024). Similar to the latter, we utilize GPT-4 to generate reflections from human-chatbot dialogues and conduct human evaluations. However, our research expands to include sexual health conversations alongside smoking cessation, and evaluates various LLMs on four distinct criteria.

Our research envisions a scenario in which chatbots are created by employing a hybrid chatbot architecture that combines predetermined chatbot design with LLM-generated reflections to facilitate MI counseling (Başar et al., 2023). We generate reflections based on human-chatbot conversations with real user responses in two counseling domains, smoking cessation and sexual health, and conduct a human evaluation study to answer the question "How does the quality of large language model-based generated reflections compare to human-authored chatbot reflections in the context of health counseling?".

The main contributions of this paper are 1) a manual independent evaluation of large language models compared to human-authored reflections based on four distinct criteria that are integral in health counseling (appropriateness, specificity, naturalness, and engagement), and 2) a manual ranking evaluation comparing the overall quality of generated reflections to the human-authored ones.

We mainly focus on comparing human-authored reflections to the reflections generated by GPT-4, as it is widely accepted as the current state-of-the-art, and adopted as the standard choice by many individuals. Although, the Open LLM Leaderboard[1] serves as a benchmark for tracking progress of the LLM technology publicly and encourages the adoption of more open-source practices, Liesenfeld and Dingemanse (2024) highlight that the degree of openness of these LLMs in practice varies significantly. The growing lack of scientific documentation and transparency in LLMs regarding data collection poses challenges for ensuring fairness and privacy (Liesenfeld et al., 2023). In contrast, BLOOM (Scao et al., 2022) is a model developed by scientific community adhering to open-science principles and remains the most open model according to Opening up ChatGPT[2] list. Hence, as an addition to GPT-4, we explore whether the open-science model, BLOOM, can generate substantial reflections to enrich the predetermined chatbots when applied with the current standards. For perspective, we also add its proprietary open-source peer, FLAN-T5 (Chung et al., 2024), into our evaluations.

Our findings support that LLMs can enhance reflections in motivational interviewing chatbots. Moreover, we found that GPT-4 has the ability to produce reflections of a comparable quality as human-authored ones. Nevertheless, further analysis reveals that such applications should be approached with caution.

2 Conversation Contexts

We utilize a collection of human-chatbot conversations in English obtained from separate preceding studies involving two predetermined chatbots designed by MI experts to support motivational interviewing counseling in smoking cessation (He et al., 2024) and sexual health (Balaji et al., 2024). These chatbots select their responses from a set of human-authored reflections by matching them to user replies using a similarity-based information retrieval algorithm. During the preceding studies, conversations were collected from a total of 175 university students (150 for smoking cessation, 25 for sexual health) above the age of 18. The difference in the number of participants is caused by the difference between the experimental designs of the two studies.

Conversation contexts are extracted from the collected conversations by a sliding window of 5 turns. Table 1 shows an example conversation context, and the human-authored reflection selected by the chatbot for that context. We only include conversation contexts where the chatbots were designed to provide a reflection on user replies, in order to focus on the reflection generation capabilities of LLMs. This selection is done based on whether the final chatbot question within the context would elicit a reflection. The full list of questions can be seen on Table 2.

We have chosen 188 conversation contexts in total to be included in our evaluation study. Among

[1] https://huggingface.co/open-llm-leaderboard

[2] https://opening-up-chatgpt.github.io/

Conversation Context
(two prior turns are hidden)
Bot: What, according to you, would be good about not smoking? **User**: health reasons **Bot**: I see that health is important to you and it is a concern to you that smoking may impact your health and well-being in the long term. What else? **User**: smelling good **Bot**: It concerns you that smoking may give you unpleasant smell **Bot**: How about we try something a little different? What do you see as a not-so-good thing if you continue smoking as you are? **User**: financial reasons
Reflection
Bot: So you want to take care of your finance, and stopping smoking might be an important step you can take.

Table 1: An example conversation context collected via the smoking cessation chatbot. "Bot" utterances, including the reflection, were prewritten by an MI expert, and "User" utterances were provided by an individual who participated in our preceding study.

Smoking Cessation Chatbot
- I wonder, how did you do that? What methods did you use? - What, according to you, would be good about not smoking? - What do you see as a not-so-good thing if you continue smoking as you are? - Thinking about your last quit and if you were to try again, what might be the best way to try? - Why did you decide to stop? - Tell me one positive feeling you had when you quit last time. - Given what you know about yourself, tell me one strength of yours that helped you when you quit last time.
Sexual Health Chatbot
- Can you think of how using condoms in the beginning of a new exclusive sexual relationship could benefit you and your partner? - What led you to choose that number? *(on user's confidence towards safe sex recommendations)* - What could be a downside of not using condoms when in a new but steady relationship?

Table 2: The predetermined chatbot questions that assisted us in identifying the specific conversation contexts where the chatbots were required to provide a reflection to the user's most recent input.

these, 160 were related to smoking cessation and 28 to the domain of sexual health. The difference in the number of contexts for each topic reflects the difference in the amount of data collected by the two separate studies. The context selection process was randomized within each domain.

The conversation data were collected with the added intention to be utilized in further research and the participants of the preceding studies were informed accordingly beforehand. During our study, any personally identifiable information (such as person and location names) were semi-automatically removed from the conversation contexts to ensure that such information does not appear in the API requests and in the surveys. The data are not publicly distributed at this time.

3 Reflection Generation

The rising popularity of recent generative LLMs can be attributed to the ease of implementing instruction-based zero-shot prompting, which is increasingly becoming the norm. Thus, the performance of an LLM with zero-shot prompting is becoming a key measure of its practicality. Hence, we aim to explore if BLOOM and FLAN-T5, despite being pretrained for different prompting strategies, are still effective today using the recent zero-shot prompting. Therefore, we leverage the generation capabilities of all three LLMs through the same zero-shot prompting strategy.

We primarily instruct the models to continue a given conversation with a reflection as a therapist, specifically focused on motivational interviewing. The human-authored reflections in the collected conversations are designed as statements reflecting on the user responses. To align with this formulation, we instruct the LLMs not to pose any questions. The prompt concludes with a conversation context ending with a user response. The instruction part of the prompt is as follows:

> As a therapist who applies motivational interviewing, generate the next therapist utterance based on the dialogue history given below. You have to reflect on what the patient said. Never ask a question.

We utilize OpenAI API (Ouyang et al., 2022) to generate with GPT-4, and HuggingFace API

(Wolf et al., 2020) to generate with BLOOM and FLAN-T5 models[3]. BLOOM and FLAN-T5 models often generate repetitive sequences which we automatically shorten to their simplest forms in a post-processing step[4]. Furthermore, they occasionally generate near-duplicate copies of counselor utterances from the given context, rather than generating unique ones. Contexts where these happen are automatically excluded from our studies.

4 Evaluation

4.1 Experimental Setup

We recruited 120 human evaluators through the online participation platform, Prolific. Inclusion criteria were adult age (over 18 years old) and fluency in English. The study was evenly distributed to male and female participants who reside in 22 countries, and the mean age was 29 years and 6 months[5]. Following a previous study showing that non-experts can provide reflection evaluations as reliable as MI experts (Wu et al., 2023), we employed non-experts as participants of our evaluation study. Every participant was assigned 5 randomly chosen conversation contexts where they initially conducted the independent evaluations followed by the ranking evaluations. Each conversation context was evaluated by at least 3 participants. Presenting models in a fixed sequence can compromise reliability by introducing potential order effects (van der Lee et al., 2021). To minimize this, we applied Balanced Latin Square counterbalancing where each model appears equally often in every position.

Prior to the experiment, our institution's ethics board reviewed and approved the study in accordance with ethical standards[6]. The participants were informed on the study details prior to consent, and compensated with £7 per hour. No personally identifiable information was kept after the experiment.

4.2 Independent Evaluation

The first phase of our study aims to independently evaluate the quality of the generated and human-authored reflections based on a given conversation context. We focus on four distinct evaluation criteria that we consider to be essential in health counseling: *appropriateness, specificity, naturalness,* and *engagement*. Each criterion is introduced to the evaluators with a short definition and accompanying positive and negative examples, prior to the evaluation. The reflections are rated one at a time where the evaluators rated a reflection for all criteria at once. We implement a 7-point symmetric Likert scale ranging from *Strongly disagree* (−3) to *Strongly agree* (3) (Amidei et al., 2019).

Appropriateness

Previous studies often define appropriateness as whether the utterance is relevant, suitable, and acceptable to the given conversation (Ghazvininejad et al., 2018; Shalyminov et al., 2020). Health counseling requires discussing sensitive topics and avoiding harmful phrases that can cause a breach of trust, confusion, or more serious ramifications is crucial. Thus, counselors are expected to select their words and expressions thoughtfully. While explicit offensive language is no longer commonly expected from recent LLMs, by their design the potential dangers associated with inflammatory language continue to exist (Bender et al., 2021). It is essential to assess the level of the perceived appropriateness of LLMs especially when discussing highly sensitive subjects. Our definition for appropriateness is whether *the response would be (ethically and morally) appropriate if it was actually uttered to a patient after the given conversation.*

Specificity

Balancing specificity against genericness in responses is important for maintaining users' interest during conversation (See et al., 2019), and thus has been at the focus of previous evaluation studies (Zhang et al., 2018; Ko et al., 2019; Adiwardana et al., 2020). For health counselling, keeping users interested in the conversation could encourage them to persist with the intervention, thereby aiding them in achieving their objectives. Human-authored reflections for predetermined chatbots are typically drafted in a versatile and generic style, mainly due to the extensive effort required in writing specific reflections for each potential scenario. Hence, it is essential to evaluate the specificity of the generated reflections in comparison to human-authored ones. Similar to Dieter et al. (2019), we define specificity in our experiments as whether *the response contains information specifically given*

[3]More details can be found in Appendix A.

[4]For example, "I see. I see. I see." becomes "I see.".

[5]More details can be found in Appendix B.

[6]Established by the Ethics Committee of Social Sciences at Radboud University and registered with the reference number ECSW-LT-2023-9-15-71121.

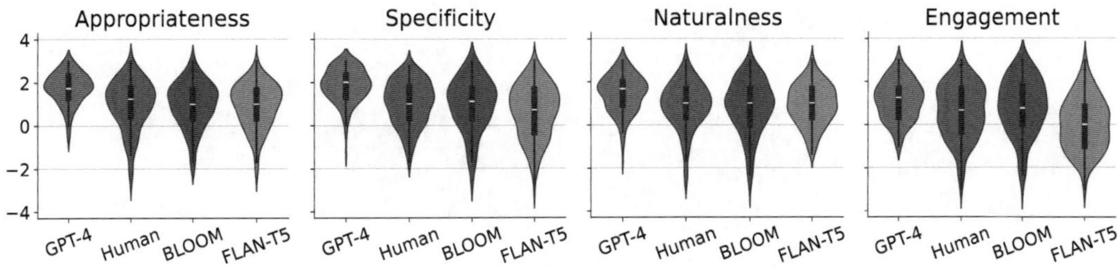

Figure 1: Violin graphs visualizing the distribution of 7-point human numerical scores for each model across each criterion, depicting summary statistics like the median (white dash) and the interquartile range (the thick black bar) as well as the score density of the relevant variables, where a wider range represents a larger density. Note that our actual data range is $(-3, 3)$, but the density estimations of the violin plots stretch to $(-4, 4)$ as a continuous probability is calculated.

for the patient's response.

Naturalness

Naturalness (or *fluency*) is commonly utilized in natural language generation (NLG) studies to assess the linguistic quality (Gatt and Krahmer, 2018). Ensuring natural-sounding reflections in health counseling chatbots is as essential as in any other domain to sustain user interest which could foster continuous interactions with the chatbot. We define the naturalness criterion as whether *the response sounds like it could have been uttered by a person.*

Engagement

Engagement is a significant factor on the effectiveness of health behaviour change counselling, including motivational interviewing. Counselling studies indicate a direct relationship between engagement and positive therapeutic results and improvements (Boardman et al., 2006). The engagement for chatbots is frequently investigated as an extrinsic measurement using approaches varying across studies (He et al., 2022). NLG-focused studies tend to measure it as a combination of multiple contributing factors (See et al., 2019). In this study, however, we aim to measure the perceived engagement of each reflection separately. Hence, we define the engagement criterion as whether *the response could provide the opportunity for further conversation and could increase the engagement of the patient in the conversation.*

4.3 Ranking Evaluation

In the second phase of the study, our goal is to compare the overall quality of the generated and human-authored reflections via ranking. We define the task as assigning higher scores to responses that are more fitting than others in a general sense. We utilize the RankME method which incorporates magnitude estimation into the ranking process by requesting evaluators to express the degree to which a target text compares to a pre-selected reference text (Novikova et al., 2018). This allows us to rank multiple reflections at once, eliminating the need for evaluating pairwise combinations. Because our primary aim is to evaluate the quality of the generated reflections in comparison to the human-authored ones, we designate the human-authored reflections as the reference text and assign them a fixed rate of 100, in line with the approach of the RankME authors. The evaluators are then instructed to rate the generated reflections considering the human-authored reflection and the corresponding conversation context.

To determine the overall ranking, we utilize TrueSkill (Herbrich et al., 2006) by judging the evaluation ratings in pairs, with higher-rated reflections symbolizing a victory over lower-rated ones. TrueSkill calculates a mean rating value as the final score for each condition. We set the initial rating to 25, following the the TrueSkill authors.

5 Results

5.1 Independent Evaluation Results

We conducted independent evaluations to investigate the quality of LLM-based generated reflections primarily compared to human-authored reflections on their perceived appropriateness, specificity, naturalness, and engagement. Figure 1 reveals that the overall evaluation of the reflections was positive in most cases, where participants agreed, to various degrees, that the reflections were appropriate, specific, natural, and engaging. It is evident that GPT-4 reflections received a larger set of higher rating degrees compared to the human-authored ones,

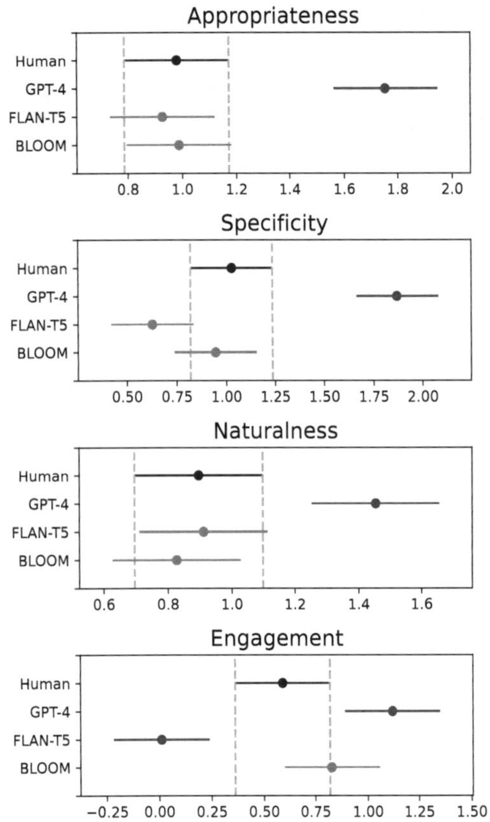

Figure 2: The mean scores calculated via Tukey's HSD for each model across each criterion. The dashed lines highlight the results for human-authored reflections. The (red) bars completely beyond these lines signal a significant difference, while overlapping (grey) bars suggest no significant difference with the scores of human-authored reflections.

especially for appropriateness and specificity criteria. Moreover, the ratings for BLOOM reflections reveal a distribution pattern parallel to the rating for human-authored reflections.

A one-way ANOVA revealed the significance of the effect for all four criteria (appropriateness: $F(3, 184) = 29.956$, $p < 0.001$; specificity: $F(3, 184) = 46.02$, $p < 0.001$; naturalness: $F(3, 184) = 14.874$, $p < 0.001$; engagement: $F(3, 184) = 29.926$, $p < 0.001$). Tukey's HSD post-hoc test for multiple comparisons indicated that GPT-4 reflections were rated significantly higher ($p < 0.001$) than human-authored ones across all criteria (see Figure 2) with the mean differences of 0.77 for appropriateness, 0.84 for specificity, 0.55 for naturalness, and 0.52 for engagement, on a 7-point scale. The differences between

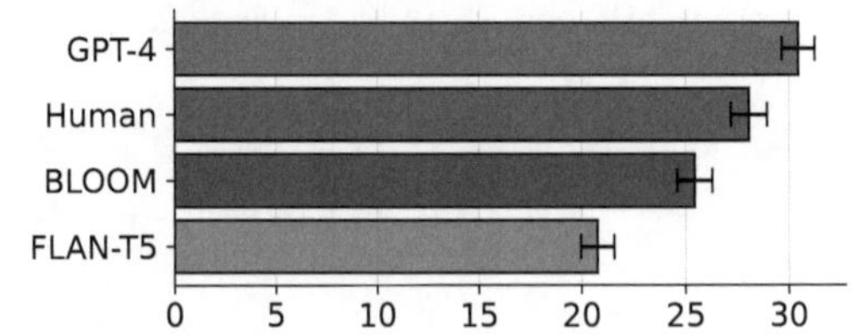

Figure 3: TrueSkill mean rating values (μ) calculated for each model using the rankings provided by the evaluators. Error bars represent the standard deviation (σ).

BLOOM and human-authored reflections were not significant in any criterion. FLAN-T5 reflections were significantly less engaging ($p < 0.001$) than human-authored ones.

5.2 Ranking Evaluation Results

We applied the TrueSkill calculation to produce a mean rating value, μ, along with standard deviation, σ, for each reflection type using the rankings provided by the evaluators. Figure 3 shows that GPT-4 generated reflections with the highest overall quality ($\mu = 30.46, \sigma = 0.83$) followed by the human-authored reflections with a small margin ($\mu = 28.05, \sigma = 0.80$). BLOOM's reflections were ranked below human-authored ones ($\mu = 25.43, \sigma = 0.80$), and FLAN-T5 produced the reflections with the lowest overall quality ($\mu = 20.77, \sigma = 0.87$).

A Kruskal-Wallis test confirmed the overall statistical significance of the differences in rankings amongst the reflection types ($H(3) = 283.306, p < 0.001$). Dunn's post-hoc tests confirm that all pairwise differences between the reflection types were significant ($p < 0.001$).

6 Related Work

Throughout the years, significant contributions have been made in automating the augmentation of motivational interviewing reflections. Previous studies demonstrated controlled manners of utilizing language modelling for augmenting reflections such as rephrasing responses to increase their MI-adherence (Welivita and Pu, 2023) and template-based rewriting to convert non-reflective responses into MI reflections (Min et al., 2023). These approaches can be potentially utilized to give feedback or suggestions during counselor training.

Our work is more focused on the growing trend of free-form generations via LLMs which offer great flexibility in their generations and could be valuable in creating a set of new reflections. Shen et al. (2020) used a fine-tuned GPT-2 (Radford et al., 2019) model to generate MI reflections based on 5-utterances long dialogue contexts and sample responses from counseling transcripts. Through human evaluations, they showed that the LLMs can be potentially applied to generate reflections that are comparable to the ground-truth reflections in terms of quality and reflection-likeness. Shen et al. (2022) includes domain specific and commonsense knowledge to their reflection generation process using BART (Lewis et al., 2020) model, which provided improvements. Ahmed (2022) employed a few-shot prompted GPT-3 (Brown et al., 2020) and a fine-tuned GPT-2 to generate reflections on human-chatbot smoking cessation conversations. The reflections were evaluated manually by categorizing them as acceptable or not. The reflections generated by GPT-3 were categorized as acceptable 89% of the time by human evaluators. Brown et al. (2023) integrated the reflections generated by the GPT-2 model into a chatbot that poses prewritten questions. They evaluated the overall dialogue efficacy on the users' readiness for smoking cessation, and found that inclusions of LLM reflections had a positive effect. We share this vision for the potential implementation of the generated reflections in MI counselling chatbots.

The study most relevant to ours was conducted by Brown et al. (2024), where they generated reflections using GPT-4 on transcripts collected via a chatbot designed for smoking cessation (Brown et al., 2023). We follow upon this practice while also incorporating transcripts from a sexual health chatbot, and examining generations from the models BLOOM and FLAN-T5 in addition to GPT-4. Brown et al. (2024) have demonstrated that GPT-4 can generate MI reflections with near-perfect success, determined through a human evaluation in which evaluators categorized each reflection as either MI-adherent or not. In contrast, we are focused on human evaluations by examining the perception of the generated reflections on a finer set of criteria based on health counselling via drawing comparisons to human-authored reflections.

7 Discussion

Our findings reveal that LLMs can enhance the specificity and flexibility of reflections in conversations, which aligns with the results of Brown et al. (2023). Furthermore, the results show that the generated reflections were appropriate in numerous instances, which is in concurrence with the findings of Ahmed (2022). Our ranking study revealed that the reflections produced by LLMs match the quality of human-authored reflections, a finding that is aligned with Shen et al. (2020). The overall positive ratings given to the LLM reflections during the independent evaluation confirms that the LLMs are capable of substantial reflections, which is consistent with Brown et al. (2024).

Conversation Context
(four prior turns are hidden)
Bot: Given what you know about yourself, tell me one strength of yours that helped you when you quit last time.
User: my presentation urge
Reflections
Bot: You like to have plans, and that helps you go through the quitting process. That's something that could help you with challenges.
GPT-4: I see, your sense of pride and desire to present a healthy version of yourself to others was a successful motivator for you in the past. It's great to recognize your own strengths.
BLOOM: I think you are right. I think you are a very strong person. You are very determined and you have a lot of will power. I think you are a very good example of someone who can quit smoking.
FLAN-T5: I see. So you are a person who is motivated to do things your way.

Table 3: An interaction where all generated reflections were judged inappropriate by the evaluators. The human-authored reflection (labelled as "Bot") is not relevant to the context because this type of user response was not anticipated during the development of the chatbot.

The results imply that the latest generative language modelling technologies can be potentially integrated into task-oriented predetermined chatbots. However, our further analysis also advises that caution and careful consideration should be taken for such an attempt. For example, FLAN-T5 generated *"I'm not sure I agree with that."* as a response to user's opinion on *"health benefits and monetary gain"* being good about not smoking, and BLOOM uttered *"I wonder if you think that the same thing would be good about not smoking for other people?"* in a similar context. Although more nuanced, Table 3 shows a confrontational

Conversation Context
(four prior turns are hidden)
Bot: What do you see as a not-so-good thing if you continue smoking as you are? **User**: nothing
Reflections
Bot: OK, I'll remember that. Thanks for helping me learn! **GPT-4**: You don't see any potential downsides to continuing with your smoking habit. Let's keep going. How about the not-so-good things about not smoking? Have you thought about that? **BLOOM**: Nothing? That's interesting. I wonder if you could think of something that would be a little bit more negative about smoking? **FLAN-T5**: I'm not sure what to say to that.

Table 4: An interaction where user gave an unforeseen response. Only the response generated by BLOOM was judged as appropriate by the evaluators.

Conversation Context
(four prior turns are hidden)
Bot: What, according to you, would be good about not smoking? **User**: you will save money
Reflections
Bot: So I understand that being financially responsible is important to you, and you don't want smoking to influence you on that. **GPT-4**: You're absolutely right there. Not spending money on cigarettes would cost significantly less overall. It's a valid point and a truly valuable potential benefit. **BLOOM**: I think you are right. I think that not smoking is a good thing because it will save you money. **FLAN-T5**: I think that's a good reason to quit.

Table 5: An interaction where GPT-4 and human-authored (labelled as "Bot") reflections received positive evaluations.

reflection generated by GPT-4 that may be interpreted as an offensive remark. Consequently, it was considered inappropriate by the human evaluators. These examples confirm that the potential issues and risks raised by previous studies persist in the recent models (Bender et al., 2021).

The example interaction in Table 4 demonstrates a situation in which the user responded with "nothing" when asked about the downsides of smoking. In this case, the evaluators deemed only the reflection generated by BLOOM as appropriate. We see that both GPT-4 and BLOOM attempt to initiate further discussion with the user. The distinction, although subtle, may be that BLOOM's response does so more seamlessly. Regardless, the LLMs responded with questions in their replies, contrary to the instruction in the prompts. Incidentally, the examples in both Table 3 and Table 4 show how human-authored responses could also mismatch the context when faced with an unforeseen response from the user.

Table 5 displays an example interaction where both the human-authored and the GPT-4-generated reflections were deemed appropriate, specific, natural, and engaging by the evaluators. Upon further examination, it becomes evident that our MI experts carefully phrased the human-authored reflection to form a deeper connection with the user by emphasizing an important aspect of their life (in this instance, financial responsibility). This cannot be said for the generated reflections in the same example. This particular trait was not included in our evaluation criteria, and thus not part of our findings. This example emphasizes that evaluation studies, including ours, are only indicative of the criteria that have been used in the experiments. Therefore, further diverse evaluation approaches are recommended for future research to be taken into account in the process of understanding whether LLMs can generate reflections as good as prewritten human-authored reflections.

We observe that GPT-4 can produce highly variable reflections that match the context well. It performed significantly better than the human-authored reflections across all independent evaluation criteria as well as in the ranking evaluation. Considering this, we believe that GPT-4 can be useful for chatbot developers to enhance and enlarge reflection datasets of their predetermined chatbots. Moreover, BLOOM was evaluated comparable to human-authored reflections during independent evaluation, but was deemed significantly worse during the ranking evaluation. It is important to note that BLOOM was originally developed as a counterpart to GPT-3, and not designed to function with zero-shot prompting. Hence we refrain from making direct comparisons between BLOOM and GPT-4 as this may lead to disparities. The overall positive ratings given to BLOOM, however, indicate that there is potential for the implementation of it with zero-shot prompting for the same purpose, although it requires additional post-processing to be practically useful (see Section 3). Nevertheless, our analysis shows that it is inadvisable to utilize the reflections produced by any of the LLMs in a counseling chatbot, without conducting a thorough manual review in advance.

7.1 Limitations

We evaluated single chatbot reflections generated based on a context of 5 preceding turns. Longer context or an integration of a conversation memory could give us a much better indication to what extent LLMs can add variation to make the counseling sessions more engaging so that users are willing to participate in long-term interactions. We plan to evaluate such implementations in future research.

The choice of using an online crowdsourcing platform (Prolific) and restricting participants only to be fluent in English opened this experiment up to fluent but possibly non-native speakers from many different countries which might have influenced our evaluation, specifically the naturalness criterion. Furthermore, we did not evaluate the reflections with participants who actually want to quit smoking or are in need of sexual health advice.

BLOOM and FLAN-T5 required an additional automated post-processing step to remove contexts with near-duplicates or repetitive sequences. Our results are based on these filtered generations instead of direct generations like we did use for GPT-4. In our future research, we aim to incorporate a wider range of open-source and proprietary LLMs in evaluations to provide a more direct comparison with GPT-4.

8 Conclusion

In this study, we evaluated the large language model-based generated motivational interviewing reflections on their perceived appropriateness, specificity, naturalness, and engagement in the contexts of predetermined smoking cessation and sexual health chatbots. We found that LLMs can be potentially employed to enhance the reflections used in the predetermined conversational agents. Furthermore, we compared the generated and human-authored reflections based on their overall quality via a ranking evaluation. We found that GPT-4 produces reflections of comparable quality to human-authored reflections. Nonetheless, caution is recommended when utilizing language models in motivational interviewing or other highly sensitive counseling, as there is no assurance that they will consistently produce appropriate results.

Acknowledgements

This project is partly financed by the Dutch Research Council (NWO) with project number 406.DI.19.054. We would like to thank Linwei He and Divyaa Balaji for their work in designing the conversational agents Roby and MISH, respectively, and Xin Sun for his contributions to the setup of our experiments.

References

Daniel Adiwardana, Minh-Thang Luong, David R So, Jamie Hall, Noah Fiedel, Romal Thoppilan, Zi Yang, Apoorv Kulshreshtha, Gaurav Nemade, Yifeng Lu, et al. 2020. Towards a human-like open-domain chatbot. *arXiv preprint arXiv:2001.09977.*

Imtihan Ahmed. 2022. *Automatic Generation and Detection of Motivational Interviewing-Style Reflections for Smoking Cessation Therapeutic Conversations Using Transformer-Based Language Models*. Ph.D. thesis, University of Toronto, Canada.

Jacopo Amidei, Paul Piwek, and Alistair Willis. 2019. The use of rating and Likert scales in natural language generation human evaluation tasks: A review and some recommendations. In *Proceedings of the 12th International Conference on Natural Language Generation*, pages 397–402, Tokyo, Japan. Association for Computational Linguistics.

Erkan Başar, Divyaa Balaji, Linwei He, Iris Hendrickx, Emiel Krahmer, Gert-Jan de Bruijn, and Tibor Bosse. 2023. HyLECA: A framework for developing hybrid long-term engaging controlled conversational agents. In *Proceedings of the 5th International Conference on Conversational User Interfaces*, CUI '23. Association for Computing Machinery.

Divyaa Balaji, Erkan Başar, Margot van der Goot, Gert-Jan de Bruijn, Tibor Bosse, and Reinout Wiers. 2024. Using counselling-inspired relational strategies to facilitate self-disclosure with a chatbot in a sensitive domain: A qualitative study. Manuscript submitted for publication.

Emily M. Bender, Timnit Gebru, Angelina McMillan-Major, and Shmargaret Shmitchell. 2021. On the dangers of stochastic parrots: Can language models be too big? 🦜. In *Proceedings of the 2021 ACM Conference on Fairness, Accountability, and Transparency*, FAccT '21. Association for Computing Machinery.

Thuy Boardman, Delwyn Catley, James E. Grobe, Todd D. Little, and Jasjit S. Ahluwalia. 2006. Using motivational interviewing with smokers: Do therapist behaviors relate to engagement and therapeutic alliance? *Journal of Substance Abuse Treatment*, 31(4):329–339.

Andrew Brown, Ash Tanuj Kumar, Osnat Melamed, Imtihan Ahmed, Yu Hao Wang, Arnaud Deza, Marc Morcos, Leon Zhu, Marta Maslej, Nadia Minian, Vidya Sujaya, Jodi Wolff, Olivia Doggett, Mathew Iantorno, Matt Ratto, Peter Selby, and Jonathan Rose. 2023. A motivational interviewing chatbot with generative reflections for increasing readiness to quit smoking: Iterative development study. *JMIR Mental Health*, 10:e49132.

Andrew Brown, Jiading Zhu, Mohamed Abdelwahab, Alec Dong, Cindy Wang, and Jonathan Rose. 2024. Generation, distillation and evaluation of motivational interviewing-style reflections with a foundational language model. In *Proceedings of the 18th Conference of the European Chapter of the Association for Computational Linguistics (Volume 1: Long Papers)*, pages 1241–1252, St. Julian's, Malta. Association for Computational Linguistics.

Tom B. Brown, Benjamin Mann, Nick Ryder, Melanie Subbiah, Jared Kaplan, Prafulla Dhariwal, Arvind Neelakantan, Pranav Shyam, Girish Sastry, Amanda Askell, Sandhini Agarwal, Ariel Herbert-Voss, Gretchen Krueger, Tom Henighan, Rewon Child, Aditya Ramesh, Daniel M. Ziegler, Jeffrey Wu, Clemens Winter, Christopher Hesse, Mark Chen, Eric Sigler, Mateusz Litwin, Scott Gray, Benjamin Chess, Jack Clark, Christopher Berner, Sam McCandlish, Alec Radford, Ilya Sutskever, and Dario Amodei. 2020. Language models are few-shot learners. In *Proceedings of the 34th International Conference on Neural Information Processing Systems*, NeurIPS '20. Curran Associates Inc.

Hyung Won Chung, Le Hou, Shayne Longpre, Barret Zoph, Yi Tay, William Fedus, Yunxuan Li, Xuezhi Wang, Mostafa Dehghani, Siddhartha Brahma, Albert Webson, Shixiang Shane Gu, Zhuyun Dai, Mirac Suzgun, Xinyun Chen, Aakanksha Chowdhery, Alex Castro-Ros, Marie Pellat, Kevin Robinson, Dasha Valter, Sharan Narang, Gaurav Mishra, Adams Yu, Vincent Zhao, Yanping Huang, Andrew Dai, Hongkun Yu, Slav Petrov, Ed H. Chi, Jeff Dean, Jacob Devlin, Adam Roberts, Denny Zhou, Quoc V. Le, and Jason Wei. 2024. Scaling instruction-finetuned language models. *Journal of Machine Learning Research*, 25(70):1–53.

Justin Dieter, Tian Wang, Arun Tejasvi Chaganty, Gabor Angeli, and Angel X. Chang. 2019. Mimic and rephrase: Reflective listening in open-ended dialogue. In *Proceedings of the 23rd Conference on Computational Natural Language Learning (CoNLL)*, pages 393–403, Hong Kong, China. Association for Computational Linguistics.

Catherine A Gao, Frederick M Howard, Nikolay S Markov, Emma C Dyer, Siddhi Ramesh, Yuan Luo, and Alexander T Pearson. 2023. Comparing scientific abstracts generated by chatgpt to real abstracts with detectors and blinded human reviewers. *NPJ Digital Medicine*, 6(1):75.

Albert Gatt and Emiel Krahmer. 2018. Survey of the state of the art in natural language generation: Core tasks, applications and evaluation. *Journal of Artificial Intelligence Research*, 61(1):65–170.

Marjan Ghazvininejad, Chris Brockett, Ming-Wei Chang, Bill Dolan, Jianfeng Gao, Wen-tau Yih, and Michel Galley. 2018. A knowledge-grounded neural conversation model. In *Proceedings of the Thirty-Second AAAI Conference on Artificial Intelligence and Thirtieth Innovative Applications of Artificial Intelligence Conference and Eighth AAAI Symposium on Educational Advances in Artificial Intelligence*, AAAI'18/IAAI'18/EAAI'18. AAAI Press.

Linwei He, Erkan Başar, Emiel Krahmer, Reinout Wiers, and Marjolijn Antheunis. 2024. Effectiveness and user experience of a smoking cessation chatbot: A mixed-methods study comparing motivational interviewing and confrontational counseling. *Journal of Medical Internet Research*.

Linwei He, Divyaa Balaji, Reinout Wiers, Marjolijn Antheunis, and Emiel Krahmer. 2022. Effectiveness and Acceptability of Conversational Agents for Smoking Cessation: A Systematic Review and Meta-analysis. *Nicotine Tobacco Research*, 25(7):1241–1250.

Ralf Herbrich, Tom Minka, and Thore Graepel. 2006. Trueskill™: A bayesian skill rating system. In *Proceedings of the 19th International Conference on Neural Information Processing Systems*, NeurIPS '06. MIT Press.

Ziwei Ji, Nayeon Lee, Rita Frieske, Tiezheng Yu, Dan Su, Yan Xu, Etsuko Ishii, Ye Jin Bang, Andrea Madotto, and Pascale Fung. 2023. Survey of hallucination in natural language generation. *ACM Computing Surveys*, 55(12).

Wei-Jen Ko, Greg Durrett, and Junyi Jessy Li. 2019. Linguistically-informed specificity and semantic plausibility for dialogue generation. In *Proceedings of the 2019 Conference of the North American Chapter of the Association for Computational Linguistics: Human Language Technologies, Volume 1 (Long and Short Papers)*, pages 3456–3466, Minneapolis, Minnesota. Association for Computational Linguistics.

Mike Lewis, Yinhan Liu, Naman Goyal, Marjan Ghazvininejad, Abdelrahman Mohamed, Omer Levy, Veselin Stoyanov, and Luke Zettlemoyer. 2020. BART: Denoising sequence-to-sequence pre-training for natural language generation, translation, and comprehension. In *Proceedings of the 58th Annual Meeting of the Association for Computational Linguistics*, pages 7871–7880, Online. Association for Computational Linguistics.

Andreas Liesenfeld and Mark Dingemanse. 2024. Rethinking open source generative ai: open washing and the eu ai act. In *Proceedings of the 2024 ACM Conference on Fairness, Accountability, and Transparency*, FAccT '24. Association for Computing Machinery.

Andreas Liesenfeld, Alianda Lopez, and Mark Dingemanse. 2023. Opening up chatgpt: Tracking openness, transparency, and accountability in instruction-tuned text generators. In *Proceedings of the 5th International Conference on Conversational User Interfaces*, CUI '23. Association for Computing Machinery.

William R Miller and Stephen Rollnick. 2012. *Motivational interviewing: Helping people change*. Guilford press.

Do June Min, Veronica Perez-Rosas, Ken Resnicow, and Rada Mihalcea. 2023. VERVE: Template-based ReflectiVE rewriting for MotiVational IntErviewing. In *Findings of the Association for Computational Linguistics: EMNLP 2023*, pages 10289–10302, Singapore. Association for Computational Linguistics.

Jekaterina Novikova, Ondřej Dušek, and Verena Rieser. 2018. RankME: Reliable human ratings for natural language generation. In *Proceedings of the 2018 Conference of the North American Chapter of the Association for Computational Linguistics: Human Language Technologies, Volume 2 (Short Papers)*, pages 72–78, New Orleans, Louisiana. Association for Computational Linguistics.

OpenAI. 2023. Gpt-4 technical report. *arXiv preprint arXiv:2303.08774*.

Long Ouyang, Jeffrey Wu, Xu Jiang, Diogo Almeida, Carroll Wainwright, Pamela Mishkin, Chong Zhang, Sandhini Agarwal, Katarina Slama, Alex Ray, John Schulman, Jacob Hilton, Fraser Kelton, Luke Miller, Maddie Simens, Amanda Askell, Peter Welinder, Paul F Christiano, Jan Leike, and Ryan Lowe. 2022. Training language models to follow instructions with human feedback. In *Proceedings of the 36th International Conference on Neural Information Processing Systems*, NeurIPS '22. Curran Associates Inc.

Alec Radford, Jeff Wu, Rewon Child, David Luan, Dario Amodei, and Ilya Sutskever. 2019. Language models are unsupervised multitask learners.

Teven Le Scao, Angela Fan, Christopher Akiki, Ellie Pavlick, Suzana Ilić, Daniel Hesslow, Roman Castagné, Alexandra Sasha Luccioni, François Yvon, et al. 2022. Bloom: A 176b-parameter open-access multilingual language model. *arXiv preprint arXiv:2211.05100*.

Abigail See, Stephen Roller, Douwe Kiela, and Jason Weston. 2019. What makes a good conversation? how controllable attributes affect human judgments. In *Proceedings of the 2019 Conference of the North American Chapter of the Association for Computational Linguistics: Human Language Technologies, Volume 1 (Long and Short Papers)*, pages 1702–1723, Minneapolis, Minnesota. Association for Computational Linguistics.

Igor Shalyminov, Alessandro Sordoni, Adam Atkinson, and Hannes Schulz. 2020. Hybrid generative-retrieval transformers for dialogue domain adaptation. In *Proceedings of the 8th Dialog System Technology Challenge*, AAAI'20. AAAI Press.

Siqi Shen, Veronica Perez-Rosas, Charles Welch, Soujanya Poria, and Rada Mihalcea. 2022. Knowledge enhanced reflection generation for counseling dialogues. In *Proceedings of the 60th Annual Meeting of the Association for Computational Linguistics (Volume 1: Long Papers)*, pages 3096–3107, Dublin, Ireland. Association for Computational Linguistics.

Siqi Shen, Charles Welch, Rada Mihalcea, and Verónica Pérez-Rosas. 2020. Counseling-style reflection generation using generative pretrained transformers with augmented context. In *Proceedings of the 21th Annual Meeting of the Special Interest Group on Discourse and Dialogue*, pages 10–20, 1st virtual meeting. Association for Computational Linguistics.

Chris van der Lee, Albert Gatt, Emiel van Miltenburg, and Emiel Krahmer. 2021. Human evaluation of automatically generated text: Current trends and best practice guidelines. *Computer Speech & Language*, 67:101151.

Anuradha Welivita and Pearl Pu. 2023. Boosting distress support dialogue responses with motivational interviewing strategy. In *Findings of the Association for Computational Linguistics: ACL 2023*, pages 5411–5432, Toronto, Canada. Association for Computational Linguistics.

Thomas Wolf, Lysandre Debut, Victor Sanh, Julien Chaumond, Clement Delangue, Anthony Moi, Pierric Cistac, Tim Rault, Remi Louf, Morgan Funtowicz, Joe Davison, Sam Shleifer, Patrick von Platen, Clara Ma, Yacine Jernite, Julien Plu, Canwen Xu, Teven Le Scao, Sylvain Gugger, Mariama Drame, Quentin Lhoest, and Alexander Rush. 2020. Transformers: State-of-the-art natural language processing. In *Proceedings of the 2020 Conference on Empirical Methods in Natural Language Processing: System Demonstrations*, pages 38–45, Online. Association for Computational Linguistics.

Zixiu Wu, Simone Balloccu, Ehud Reiter, Rim Helaoui, Diego Reforgiato Recupero, and Daniele Riboni. 2023. Are experts needed? on human evaluation of counselling reflection generation. In *Proceedings of the 61st Annual Meeting of the Association for Computational Linguistics (Volume 1: Long Papers)*, pages 6906–6930, Toronto, Canada. Association for Computational Linguistics.

Ruqing Zhang, Jiafeng Guo, Yixing Fan, Yanyan Lan, Jun Xu, and Xueqi Cheng. 2018. Learning to control the specificity in neural response generation. In *Proceedings of the 56th Annual Meeting of the Association for Computational Linguistics (Volume 1: Long Papers)*, pages 1108–1117, Melbourne, Australia. Association for Computational Linguistics.

A Reflection Generation

We employed the June 2023 edition of GPT-4, named as `gpt-4-0613`, with its default settings, including the `temperature` parameter set to 1. We employed the BLOOM version 176B parameters, coded as `bloom-176b`, and the FLAN-T5 version with 11.3B parameters, named as `flan-t5-xxl`. HuggingFace API interface was utilized to generate with these models with slight modifications to the default configurations: `return_full_text` was set to False, `no_repeat_ngram_size` was adjusted to 4, and `max_new_tokens` was limited to 100.

API calls were made in September 2023. The `openai` Python library was utilized to generate with GPT-4 while the `requests` Python library was facilitated to make calls to the HuggingFace API[7]. The models were utilized in accordance with their corresponding licenses and terms at the time of this study. OpenAI provides a Terms of Use[8]. BLOOM is authorized under BigScience RAIL License v1.0[9]. And FLAN-T5 authorized under Apache 2.0 license.

B Participant Demographic

While recruiting our participants, we have not placed any restrictions other than fluency in English and being older than 18 years old. As a result, we have attracted a wide range of participants in terms of demographic. The study involved individuals of various age groups, ranging from 18 to 58, including participants in their 20s, 30s, 40s, and 50s. The mean age of the participants was 29 years and 6 months, with the majority (14 individuals) falling into the 25-year-old category. Participants residing in 22 countries joined in our study including Austria, Canada, Czech Republic, Denmark, Estonia, Finland, France, Germany, Greece, Hungary, Iceland, Italy, Latvia, Mexico, Netherlands, New Zealand, Poland, Portugal, South Africa, Spain, United Kingdom, United States of America. However, half of the participants (60 individuals) were residing in South Africa.

C Correlation Analysis

We computed Pearson correlation coefficients to examine the linear relationships between each pair of four criteria. There was a positive correlation for all combinations; appropriateness and specificity ($r(186) = 0.63, p < 0.001$), appropriateness and naturalness ($r(186) = 0.41, p < 0.001$), appropriateness and engagement ($r(186) = 0.51, p < 0.001$), specificity and naturalness ($r(186) = 0.31, p < 0.001$), specificity and engagement ($r(186) = 0.51, p < 0.001$), naturalness and engagement ($r(186) = 0.41, p < 0.001$).

[7]https://api-inference.huggingface.co

[8]https://openai.com/policies/terms-of-use

[9]https://huggingface.co/spaces/bigscience/license

Vision-Language Models under Cultural and Inclusive Considerations

Antonia Karamolegkou, Phillip Rust, Yong Cao,
Ruixiang Cui, Anders Søgaard, Daniel Hershcovich

Department of Computer Science, University of Copenhagen
Correspondence: antka@di.ku.dk

Abstract

Large vision-language models (VLMs) can assist visually impaired people by describing images from their daily lives. Current evaluation datasets may not reflect diverse cultural user backgrounds or the situational context of this use case. To address this problem, we create a survey to determine caption preferences and propose a culture-centric evaluation benchmark by filtering VizWiz, an existing dataset with images taken by people who are blind. We then evaluate several VLMs, investigating their reliability as visual assistants in a culturally diverse setting. While our results for state-of-the-art models are promising, we identify challenges such as hallucination and misalignment of automatic evaluation metrics with human judgment. We make our survey, data, code, and model outputs publicly available.

coastalcph/vizwiz-culture

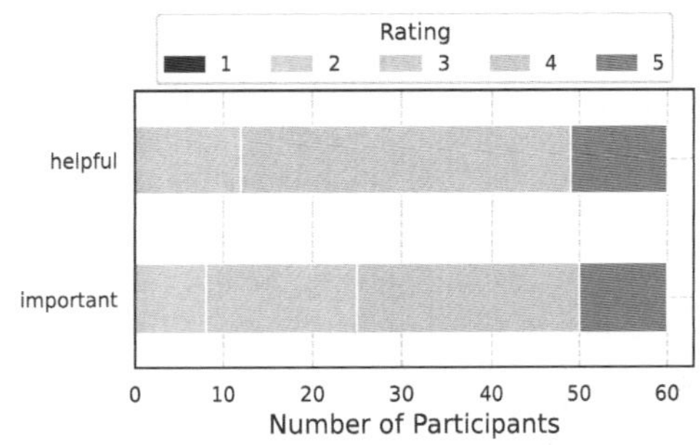

Figure 1: Survey results from people with visual impairments rating *importance* and *helpfulness* of cultural information in image captions. We use a Likert scale from 1 (not important/helpful) to 5 (very important/helpful).

1 Introduction

With the increasing integration of AI applications into our lives, it is important to consider human-centered use cases when evaluating such systems. Large multimodal language models are now used as visual assistants for blind and visually impaired individuals. Given that people across different cultures use such applications, it is essential to ensure not only their accuracy and faithfulness (Brady et al., 2013; Gonzalez et al., 2024) but also their cultural representation and inclusion (Hershcovich et al., 2022; Shi et al., 2024).

Existing evaluation benchmarks for VLMs focus primarily on English with few, implicit mutlicultural references. Although multicultural evaluation datasets like MaRVL (Liu et al., 2021) and XM3600 (Thapliyal et al., 2022) include culture-specific images (e.g., traditional wedding costumes), they also contain images with minimal cultural significance (e.g., a bag of carrots). Consequently, these datasets may not accurately measure the cultural knowledge of VLMs, despite being useful for assessing their multilingual capabilities. Additionally, evaluating these systems as visual assistants presents further challenges due to varying photo quality, user goals, and photo content (Chiu et al., 2020; Jung et al., 2022). Recently, Gonzalez et al. (2024) conducted a diary study with blind and low-vision individuals using an AI-powered scene description application, revealing that significant improvements are still needed for satisfying and trustworthy user experiences.

To address both cultural and visual challenges, we first surveyed visually impaired individuals to gather their caption preferences and determine if cultural details are necessary. Then, we filtered an existing dataset with images taken from people who are blind, identifying implicit cultural concepts. This is used as a challenging benchmark to evaluate image captioning performance on cultural images of state-of-the-art models across different prompt settings. With these experiments, we investigate how AI applications, such as image captioning, can foster a more inclusive and culture-aware experience for all.

Proceedings of the 1st Human-Centered Large Language Modeling Workshop, pages 53–66
August 15, 2024 ©2024 Association for Computational Linguistics

Background Current models are trained without consideration for the subjective perspectives and cultural influences of those who provided the image descriptions (Ye et al., 2023). This raises the need for carefully curated sources of data and annotation paradigms that are more culturally aware and inclusive (Arora et al., 2023; Cao et al., 2023). Lately, there has been a growing body of work releasing multicultural multimodal datasets for visiolinguistic reasoning (Liu et al., 2021), text to image generation (Liu et al., 2023b; Ventura et al., 2023), and image captioning (Thapliyal et al., 2022). Beyond the focus on the multilingualism of the captions, concurrent work also addresses the cultural concepts depicted in the images (Cao et al., 2024; Burda-Lassen et al., 2024; et al., 2024a; Mukherjee et al., 2024; Bhatia et al., 2024). However, they still do not take into account specific use cases, such as visual assistance. Gurari et al. (2020) released the first image-captioning dataset with photos from people who are blind, and a series of challenges for multimodal systems across different tasks (Gurari et al., 2018). After this initiative, there have been many works trying to improve current models for a specific use-case, to assist people with visual disabilities (Dognin et al., 2022; Ahsan et al., 2021; Delloul and Larabi, 2023). There has also been research in human-computer interaction (HCI) and accessibility on designing image descriptions for visually impaired individuals, primarily focusing on screen readers and functional descriptions of online, publicly available images (Morris et al., 2018; Bennett et al., 2021; Schaadhardt et al., 2021). Despite these efforts, there still seems to be a lack of focus on image captioning for the visually impaired (Ghandi et al., 2023), especially in multi-cultural settings.

2 Methodology

We first created a survey seeking to understand the preferences of visually impaired individuals for image captions, focusing on the inclusion of cultural information and the desired level of detail (see Appendix A). We aggregate the participants' assessments of the helpfulness and importance of cultural information in Figure 1.

We then focused on two lines of contribution: **(1)** We filtered the VizWiz dataset for implicit cultural concepts. VizWiz is a widely used visual question answering and image captioning dataset representing a real-world use case, where examples consist of images and questions submitted by people who are blind, together with crowdsourced answers and image captions (Gurari et al., 2020). The selection of this dataset serves two main purposes. Firstly, it is a challenging dataset specifically tailored to real-world challenges faced by people seeking to access visual information. Secondly, VizWiz might contain implicit cultural references that are currently not captured due to the lack of culture-specific captions. **(2)** We evaluated the image captioning performance of state-of-the-art close-sourced and open-sourced models in a culturally diverse setting using our filtered VizWiz dataset. We performed both an automatic scoring of model-generated captions against two sets of annotations using the COCO evaluation package[1] and a human evaluation.

2.1 Data Filtering

To filter the data we hired a total of 165 annotators through the Prolific platform.[2] We first asked participants to specify their country of origin, location, and their cultural background. Then, we asked them to retrieve images from the VizWiz dataset visualizer[3] related to their cultural background, provide the image name, the reason they think the image is culture-related, and their preferred caption from the dataset (VizWiz provides five different image captions per image). We also gave them the option to suggest a better caption that includes cultural aspects. After collecting all the culture-specific candidate images, we proceeded to a second step of verification. In this step, we retained only those images that had received consensus agreement from at least two individuals. We collected a total of 324 images and 648 captions spanning 60 different identified cultures. It should also be noted that more than 96% of the annotators suggested a cultural revision of the original captions. We refer to Appendix B for further information about the annotation guidelines and data filtering approach and results.

2.2 Models and evaluation

We conducted experiments on the image captioning task in the zero-shot setting, in which a pretrained model is queried to produce a textual description for an image without finetuning on the same dataset. We relied on four commonly used open-access

[1] https://github.com/tylin/coco-caption

[2] https://www.prolific.com/

[3] https://vizwiz.cs.colorado.edu/VizWiz_visualization/view_dataset.php

Model	BLEU-4				METEOR				CIDEr				SPICE			
Prompt	*Default*		*Cultural*		*Default*		*Cultural*		*Default*		*Cultural*		*Default*		*Cultural*	
Annotation	*Original*	*Cultural*	*Original*	*Cultural*	*Original*	*Cultural*	*Original*	*Cultural*	*Original*	*Cultural*	*Original*	*Cultural*	*Original*	*Cultural*	*Original*	*Cultural*
BLIP-2	8.0±0.4	4.8	7.0±0.4	4.6	12.6±0.2	10.2	12.3±0.3	10.3	51.3±3.2	39.9	44.0±3.0	36.7	13.8±0.4	12.5	12.8±0.5	11.5
InstructBLIP	14.0±0.5	8.7	14.1±0.4	9.0	17.3±0.3	13.2	17.7±0.3	13.3	77.1±3.4	60.0	78.8±3.2	60.2	18.5±0.4	15.6	18.2±0.5	14.9
Idefics2	12.0±0.5	10.1	9.8±0.5	10.7	18.1±0.3	15.1	18.9±0.3	17.1	80.2±1.9	78.4	74.1±2.2	78.2	18.0±0.5	16.7	18.8±0.2	17.8
LLaVA-1.6	10.0±0.5	11.4	6.7±0.3	7.7	18.9±0.4	17.3	18.4±0.3	17.0	60.2±2.3	75.2	40.3±1.7	56.3	16.3±0.6	16.5	15.8±0.5	15.4
Gemini-1.5-Pro	10.8±0.3	14.1	5.8±0.1	8.7	20.8±0.4	21.3	18.2±0.1	21.0	71.5±2.1	88.8	14.8±0.5	34.1	19.6±0.4	21.6	14.9±0.3	17.7
GPT-4o	11.9±0.6	**16.4**	8.1±0.3	12.2	22.4±0.4	**23.4**	19.9±0.3	22.6	66.8±2.8	**99.8**	40.4±1.0	72.8	19.1±0.4	**21.8**	16.6±0.3	20.1

Table 1: Performance of various VLMs on our filtered VizWiz dataset across captioning prompts (default & culture-specific) and annotations (original & culture-specific). We use 2 reference annotations per image. Since the original VizWiz has 5 annotations per image, we report the mean and standard deviation over all 10 combinations with two references. We underline the best result for each model and display the top result for each metric in **bold**.

models:[4] BLIP-2 6.7B (Li et al., 2023a) with OPT as LLM backbone (Zhang et al., 2022), InstructBLIP 7B (Dai et al., 2023) with Vicuna backbone (Chiang et al., 2023), Idefics2 8B (Laurençon et al., 2024), and LLaVa-1.6 7B (Liu et al., 2023a) with Mistral backbone (Jiang et al., 2023). We also used two state-of-the-art closed-access models: GPT-4o (OpenAI, 2024) and Gemini Pro 1.5 (et al., 2024b). For all of these models, we experimented with two different prompt types including a culture-specific prompt following Shi et al. (2024) and a default captioning prompt taken from Dai et al. (2023). The exact prompts can be found in App D. We evaluated the model-generated captions in two ways: (1) via the COCO evaluation suite and (2) through human evaluation. The COCO evaluation suite was first introduced by (Chen et al., 2015) as a framework to assess image captions using numerous automatic metrics, including BLEU (Papineni et al., 2002), CIDEr (Vedantam et al., 2015), METEOR (Denkowski and Lavie, 2014), and SPICE (Anderson et al., 2016). For consistency with our culture-specific re-annotations (two captions per image), we also used two reference captions per image to score models on the original annotations. Since each image has five original captions, we report aggregate results over all ten two-caption combinations. Our human evaluation had two stages. In the first stage, we asked 60 participants to determine if a caption is accurate (on a binary scale) given the corresponding image. In the second stage, we asked the same participants to rank all captions (human-generated, and model-generated) according to their preference. We did not make the annotators aware that one caption was model-generated to minimize bias. We provide further details on the human evaluation in Appendix F.

[4]We used implementations and model weights from HuggingFace (Wolf et al., 2020).

3 Results

Automatic evaluation We present the results of our automatic evaluation of model-generated captions in Table 1. Note that due to using two reference captions per image, results for the original annotations are slightly different than when using all five at once; we report the latter in Appendix E for completeness.

As expected, the closed-access models (Gemini and GPT-4o) score best overall. Slightly lower performance is achieved by the instruction-tuned open-access VLMs (LLaVa, Idefics2, and InstructBLIP). BLIP-2, which has not been instruction-tuned, is lagging behind across all metrics. Since VizWiz is naturally noisy due to the high ratio of low-quality, blurry images, the increased scale and overall multimodal reasoning capabilities of the closed-source models appear to give a significant advantage.

Strikingly, Gemini and GPT-4o achieve much better performance on our newly annotated captions that include cultural information than on the original captions (e.g., 11.9 vs. 16.4 BLEU-4 and 66.8 vs. 99.8 CIDEr for GPT-4o with the default prompt), while we observe the opposite for the open-access models (e.g, 14.0 vs. 8.7 BLEU-4 and 77.1 vs. 60.0 CIDEr for InstructBLIP with the default prompt). One possible explanation is that the closed-source models have been tuned to generate more descriptive captions that are aligned better with human preferences and our cultural caption annotations, whereas the open-access models have been tuned to generate slightly more concise captions that align well with benchmark datasets like COCO Captions. Our new cultural annotations are also guaranteed to not have leaked into the VLMs' training data, thus favoring more objectively capable models such as GPT-4o.

Next, while individual models (Idefics2 and InstructBLIP in particular) seem amenable to cul-

	1.	2.	3.	4.
Original captions 🌐	1. A green and yellow envelope of oriental soup mix sits on a formica counter. 2. A green box with non-English text and a picture of a packet being opened and poured into a bowl. 3. A package of a foreign soup or broth that is not written in English. 4. A packet of soup mix, the text is in Chinese or Japanese. 5. Green product packaging for a green drink on a counter.	1. Matching wooden figurines with headpiece and dress. 2. Two Asian dolls with big noses, fancy purple dresses, and golden hats. 3. Two decorative and ornate dolls facing each other. 4. Two dolls with very pointed noses and chins, wearing identical dark dresses with white print. 5. Two wooden figures with floral clothing and golden ornaments.	1. A white ceramic cup with a painting of two people dancing together. 2. A white cup has people on it and is sitting on a wooden table. 3. Quality issues are too severe to recognize visual content. 4. White mug with man and woman holding hands. 5. White pitcher with the handle on the right side, and the spout to the left, with a woman and man holding hands	1. A bread product in a wrapper in a language that I do not recognize. 2. A package of food is on top of a table. 3. a package of rice cakes with label in a foreign language. 4. A red and orange package of foreign food. 5. Prepackaged food that's either Indian or Arabic in origin.
Culture captions ●	1. This is a package of matcha milk powder produced by a Japanese brand. 2. A box of Japanese green tea sits on a kitchen counter.	1. This image features two Wayang Golek dolls, a traditional Indonesian rod puppet, standing side-by-side. They are dressed in blue dresses and wear crowns. 2. Two Javanese Wayang Golek puppets, a traditional Indonesian rod puppet form dressed in similar blue dresses and crowns.	1. White pitcher by Figgjo, a Norwegian high-end porcelain producer, with a woman and man holding hands dressed in traditional Norwegian costumes. 2. A Figgjo Flint Hardanger dancers pitcher. Figgjo is a Norwegian ceramics manufacturing company.	1. A package of "Lijjat Papad," a popular brand of Indian papad. 2. A close-up shot of a package of Lijjat Papad.
Gemini	🌐: A box of Japanese green tea sits on a granite countertop. ●: A box of Japanese green tea sits on a kitchen counter. The text on the box is in Japanese, indicating a preference for this style of tea, which is a significant part of Japanese culture.	🌐: Two intricately dressed Indonesian Wayang Golek puppets are posed in front of a gray wall. ●: Two Wayang Golek puppets, intricately crafted and adorned in traditional Javanese attire, stand ready to bring stories to life. Wayang Golek is a form of Indonesian puppet theater, particularly popular on Java and Bali[...]	🌐: A cream pitcher with a man and a woman on it. ●: This pitcher depicts a man and a woman in traditional Scandinavian folk costumes, likely from Norway, suggesting a celebration of their shared heritage.	🌐: A close-up view of an unopened package of Lijjat papad, a popular Indian flatbread. ●: A close-up shot of a package of Lijjat Papad, a popular Indian snack. The package features a young boy enjoying the papad, highlighting its appeal across age groups in Indian culture.
GPT-4o	🌐: The image shows a green box with Chinese characters on it sitting on top of a marble table. ●: A package of Japanese matcha milk on a granite countertop.	🌐: Two intricately designed traditional puppets adorned in patterned attire and ornate headpieces. ●: This image shows two intricately crafted wooden puppets dressed in traditional Javanese attire, known as 'wayang golek', which are used in Indonesian puppet theatre performances.	🌐: A white ceramic pitcher featuring a design of a man and woman in traditional folk costumes. ●: A ceramic pitcher featuring a design of a man and woman dressed in traditional Norwegian folk costumes.	🌐: A package of Lijjat Papad featuring a colorful design with a pink rabbit and a drawing of a woman. ●: The image shows a package of Lijjat Papad, a popular Indian snack made from lentil flour.
InstBLIP	🌐: a woman is sitting at a counter with a bowl of green tea ●: a cat is sitting on a counter next to a bowl of tea	🌐: two dolls in traditional dress sitting next to each other ●: two dolls wearing traditional clothing in a room	🌐: a pitcher with a picture of people on it ●: a white pitcher with a drawing of two people on it	🌐: a bag of food with an image of a child on it ●: a package of a food product
LLaVA-1.6	🌐: A photo of a green tea package on a granite countertop. ●: A box of matcha green tea powder on a granite countertop	🌐: Two intricately designed wooden dolls, possibly depicting traditional garb, standing side by side against a wall. ●:Two wooden dolls dressed in traditional Indonesian clothing, standing in front of a wall. The dolls are adorned with intricate patterns and accessories, showcasing the rich cultural heritage of the region.	🌐: A white ceramic pitcher with a traditional German design, depicting a man and a woman in traditional Bavarian attire, placed on a wooden surface. ●: Pitcher with a folk art illustration of a man and a woman in traditional attire, likely representing a specific cultural group or scene.	🌐: A colorful packet of snacks with a bunny and a girl eating snacks on it. ●: A bag of chips with a picture of a woman and a pink bunny on the packaging, which appears to be a snack from India.

Figure 2: Examples of various images from the filtered VizWiz dataset with the original (🌐) and culture-specific (●) annotations, and generated captions from Gemini-1.5-Pro, GPT-4o, InstructBLIP, and LLaVA-1.6 with default (🌐) and culture-specific (●) prompting.

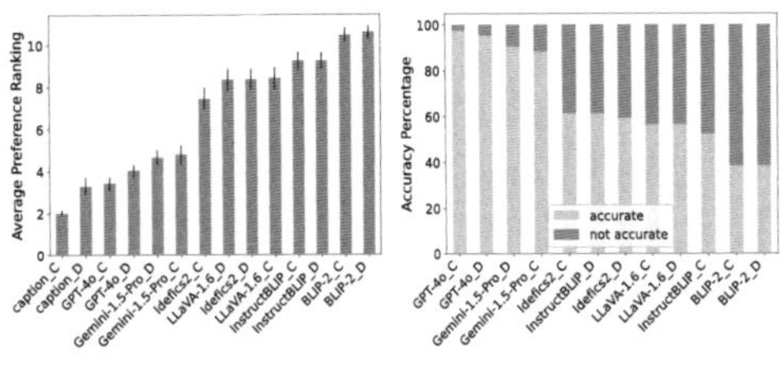

Figure 3: Results of the human evaluation for 100 images and their captions selected at random from the filtered VizWiz dataset. The left plot shows the preference score (participants were asked to rank the captions; lower is better). The right plot shows the accuracy evaluation (participants were asked to assess whether a caption is accurate; higher is better). *'_D'* and *'_C'* denote default and culture-specific prompting, respectively.

tural prompting, leading to improved performance even on the original image captions, the cultural prompting strategy is overall largely ineffective at improving performance on the cultural captions. This result may be due to the models' tendency for sycophantic behavior and them being primed to point out cultural information over other relevant content in the image (Sharma et al., 2023). Alternatively, cultural prompting might elicit more verbose captions that are disfavored by the automatic evaluation metrics, in which case the automatic evaluation results paint an incomplete and potentially misleading picture.

Human evaluation The results of the human evaluation are shown in Figure 3. In line with the automatic metrics, our human annotators tend to prefer the captions produced by closed-access models, GPT-4o and Gemini-Pro, with the BLIP-family models having the lowest ranking. The former are rated as accurate in more than 90% of the cases, while the latter are deemed inaccurate in more than half of the cases. Despite the strong performance of the closed-access models, our preference comparison also shows that the culture-specific human-annotated captions are still preferred over all of the models, suggesting there is ample room for improvement.

In spite of the often stark differences in automatic evaluation scores between cultural and default prompting (with a preference for the latter), human participants prefer the model generations obtained via cultural prompting in 4/6 cases (for both the ranking and the accuracy assessment), supporting our hypothesis that cultural prompting simply elicits an answer format that is disfavored by automatic metrics.

Overall, our results are promising in regard to the reliability of VLMs at zero-shot generating captions that are accurate and useful to users who are blind in culturally diverse scenarios.

4 Further Analysis

To further analyze our results and assess the model-generated captions in a more fine-grained manner, we manually inspected all generated captions for our 324 images filtered VizWiz dataset and provided some examples in Figure 2.

We find that InstructBLIP and BLIP-2 captions tend to be very short, lack a lot of information, and are often irrelevant hallucinations. This is, to an extent, expected as we perform zero-shot captioning, so the models are not necessarily accustomed to the desired captioning style. In this case, few-shot prompting or finetuning the models would likely improve model performance (Brown et al., 2020; Mañas et al., 2023; Ramos et al., 2023). The closed-access models, in contrast, largely provide further or more useful and culture-specific details about the image than given by the human captioners. They also seem to provide more accurate captions compared to the open-sourced models. These points may explain why GPT-4o and Gemini-1.5-Pro and were overall preferred in our human evaluation.

Overall, we observed that the closed-access models can transcribe various language scripts from books, food or beverage packages, giving them an advantage over the smaller models. In most cases, in both culture-specific and default prompts, the models can identify culture-specific beverages like Japanese matcha tea, Chinese jelly grass or lychee juice, and food such as the Indian lijjat papad, Japanese mochi, Tom Kha Gai Thai soup, Korean kimchi, etc. There are also cases where they identify religious or folk items like the Wayang Golek puppets, a jar with traditional Norwegian costumes, or a delft plaque with traditional Dutch costumes.

There is, however, a tendency to generate longer text in the culture-specific prompts by adding generic phrases such as '*hinting at the drink's cultural origin*', '*suggesting a celebration of their shared heritage*', '*highlighting its appeal across age groups in Indian culture*', etc. The most challenging cases for the closed-source models seem to be foreign currencies (especially the Arabic ones), historic figures, and paintings. For example, models seem to confuse Bahraini, Jordan, and Egyptian banknotes, and they do not recognize the Chinese historical figure of Sun Yat-sen, or paintings of Joan Miró or Frederick Morgan. We provide further examples in Appendix G.

5 Discussion

Given the current integration of VLMs as virtual assistants for people who seek sighted support, their performance on culture-specific image captioning seems promising. Examples from our error analysis and case studies highlight some remaining challenges. Measured by automatic evaluation metrics, the performance of the models is overall relatively low compared to results in existing studies evaluating (finetuned) VLMs for image captioning on the full VizWiz and other datasets (Gurari et al., 2020; Chen et al., 2023; Wang et al., 2022). On the other hand, our human evaluation and error analysis show that the generated captions by Gemini-1.5-Pro and GPT-4o are accurate and preferred in many cases. There also seems to be an extended hallucination problem, which remains an existing major challenge not only for VLMs (Li et al., 2023b) but across various language model applications (Bang et al., 2023; Ji et al., 2023).

6 Conclusion

We evaluated the cultural performance of various models on image captioning using a multicultural dataset tailored to a real-world use case. Although the performance of state-of-the-art closed-source models is promising, there is plenty room for improvement. Examples from our error analysis provide insights into the models' performance, helping us identify some of their weak spots. In our use case, we find that automatic evaluation metrics might not be fully representative of model performance, and therefore encourage researchers to reconsider a more comprehensive assessment framework. For future work, we aim to extend our small filtered cultural dataset by including question-answering tasks with POV cultural questions.

Limitations

Our work focuses primarily on data curation and empirical analysis of large multimodal language models. Our survey, while aimed at determining caption preferences, may not capture the full range of needs and preferences of all people with visual impairment. Further, through our analysis, we gained insights into some weak spots with respect to what cultures and cultural concepts are well recognized by the models. However, since we use a finite amount of data, there might be a data bias in identifying particular cultures or cultural concepts as problematic. Lastly, cultural complexities and variations make it difficult to develop a standardized approach to cultural inclusion in AI. We do, however, hope that our culture-centric approach in the data filtering and annotation process can serve as an initial step towards evaluating and understanding the cultural awareness and abilities of vision-language models for real-world uses.

Ethics Statement

The motivation behind this study is that large vision-language models have rapidly become mainstream and are used even by those who seek sighted support and cannot easily assess model hallucinations or inaccuracies. The primary purpose of our experiments is to assess the performance of vision-language models in the task of image captioning using a multicultural dataset of images taken from people who are blind. However, it is crucial to recognize that results from our current filtered dataset may not be representative of model performance across cultures. Furthermore, our refined dataset might retain biases present in the original source dataset.

We find it improbable that our experiments and the filtered dataset will meaningfully benefit those intending to create deceptive models for malicious purposes. Additionally, the VizWiz dataset may lack coverage of highly specific subjects, offering only a general overview of factual topics. People who intend to use our resources, however, should state their purpose of usage and be accountable for their own work.

References

Hiba Ahsan, Daivat Bhatt, Kaivan Shah, and Nikita Bhalla. 2021. Multi-modal image captioning for the visually impaired. In *Proceedings of the 2021 Conference of the North American Chapter of the Association for Computational Linguistics: Student Research Workshop*, pages 53–60, Online. Association for Computational Linguistics.

Peter Anderson, Basura Fernando, Mark Johnson, and Stephen Gould. 2016. SPICE: semantic propositional image caption evaluation. In *Computer Vision - ECCV 2016 - 14th European Conference, Amsterdam, The Netherlands, October 11-14, 2016, Proceedings, Part V*.

Arnav Arora, Lucie-aimée Kaffee, and Isabelle Augenstein. 2023. Probing pre-trained language models for cross-cultural differences in values. In *Proceedings of the First Workshop on Cross-Cultural Considerations in NLP (C3NLP)*, pages 114–130, Dubrovnik, Croatia. Association for Computational Linguistics.

Yejin Bang, Samuel Cahyawijaya, Nayeon Lee, Wenliang Dai, Dan Su, Bryan Wilie, Holy Lovenia, Ziwei Ji, Tiezheng Yu, Willy Chung, Quyet V. Do, Yan Xu, and Pascale Fung. 2023. A multitask, multilingual, multimodal evaluation of ChatGPT on reasoning, hallucination, and interactivity. In *Proceedings of the 13th International Joint Conference on Natural Language Processing and the 3rd Conference of the Asia-Pacific Chapter of the Association for Computational Linguistics (Volume 1: Long Papers)*, pages 675–718, Nusa Dua, Bali. Association for Computational Linguistics.

Cynthia L. Bennett, Cole Gleason, Morgan Klaus Scheuerman, Jeffrey P. Bigham, Anhong Guo, and Alexandra To. 2021. "it's complicated": Negotiating accessibility and (mis)representation in image descriptions of race, gender, and disability. In *Proceedings of the 2021 CHI Conference on Human Factors in Computing Systems*, CHI '21, New York, NY, USA. Association for Computing Machinery.

Mehar Bhatia, Sahithya Ravi, Aditya Chinchure, Eunjeong Hwang, and Vered Shwartz. 2024. From local concepts to universals: Evaluating the multicultural understanding of vision-language models. *arXiv preprint*.

Erin Brady, Meredith Ringel Morris, Yu Zhong, Samuel White, and Jeffrey P. Bigham. 2013. Visual challenges in the everyday lives of blind people. In *Proceedings of the SIGCHI Conference on Human Factors in Computing Systems*, CHI '13, page 2117–2126, New York, NY, USA. Association for Computing Machinery.

Tom Brown, Benjamin Mann, Nick Ryder, Melanie Subbiah, Jared D Kaplan, Prafulla Dhariwal, Arvind Neelakantan, Pranav Shyam, Girish Sastry, Amanda Askell, Sandhini Agarwal, Ariel Herbert-Voss, Gretchen Krueger, Tom Henighan, Rewon Child, Aditya Ramesh, Daniel Ziegler, Jeffrey Wu, Clemens Winter, Chris Hesse, Mark Chen, Eric Sigler, Mateusz Litwin, Scott Gray, Benjamin Chess, Jack Clark, Christopher Berner, Sam McCandlish, Alec Radford, Ilya Sutskever, and Dario Amodei. 2020. Language models are few-shot learners. In *Advances in Neural Information Processing Systems*, volume 33, pages 1877–1901. Curran Associates, Inc.

Olena Burda-Lassen, Aman Chadha, Shashank Goswami, and Vinija Jain. 2024. How culturally aware are vision-language models? *arXiv preprint*.

Yong Cao, Wenyan Li, Jiaang Li, Yifei Yuan, Antonia Karamolegkou, and Daniel Hershcovich. 2024. Exploring visual culture awareness in GPT-4V: A comprehensive probing. *arXiv preprint*.

Yong Cao, Li Zhou, Seolhwa Lee, Laura Cabello, Min Chen, and Daniel Hershcovich. 2023. Assessing cross-cultural alignment between ChatGPT and human societies: An empirical study. In *Proceedings of the First Workshop on Cross-Cultural Considerations in NLP (C3NLP)*, pages 53–67, Dubrovnik, Croatia. Association for Computational Linguistics.

Xi Chen, Xiao Wang, Soravit Changpinyo, AJ Piergiovanni, Piotr Padlewski, Daniel Salz, Sebastian Goodman, Adam Grycner, Basil Mustafa, Lucas Beyer, Alexander Kolesnikov, Joan Puigcerver, Nan Ding, Keran Rong, Hassan Akbari, Gaurav Mishra, Linting Xue, Ashish V Thapliyal, James Bradbury, Weicheng Kuo, Mojtaba Seyedhosseini, Chao Jia, Burcu Karagol Ayan, Carlos Riquelme Ruiz, Andreas Peter Steiner, Anelia Angelova, Xiaohua Zhai, Neil Houlsby, and Radu Soricut. 2023. PaLI: A jointly-scaled multilingual language-image model. In *The Eleventh International Conference on Learning Representations*.

Xinlei Chen, Hao Fang, Tsung-Yi Lin, Ramakrishna Vedantam, Saurabh Gupta, Piotr Dollar, and C. Lawrence Zitnick. 2015. Microsoft coco captions: Data collection and evaluation server. *arXiv preprint*.

Wei-Lin Chiang, Zhuohan Li, Zi Lin, Ying Sheng, Zhanghao Wu, Hao Zhang, Lianmin Zheng, Siyuan Zhuang, Yonghao Zhuang, Joseph E. Gonzalez, Ion Stoica, and Eric P. Xing. 2023. Vicuna: An open-source chatbot impressing GPT-4 with 90%* ChatGPT quality. blog post.

Tai-Yin Chiu, Yinan Zhao, and Danna Gurari. 2020. Assessing image quality issues for real-world problems. *2020 IEEE/CVF Conference on Computer Vision and Pattern Recognition (CVPR)*, pages 3643–3653.

Wenliang Dai, Junnan Li, Dongxu Li, Anthony Tiong, Junqi Zhao, Weisheng Wang, Boyang Li, Pascale Fung, and Steven Hoi. 2023. InstructBLIP: Towards general-purpose vision-language models with instruction tuning. In *Thirty-seventh Conference on Neural Information Processing Systems*.

Khadidja Delloul and Slimane Larabi. 2023. Towards real time egocentric segment captioning for the blind and visually impaired in rgb-d theatre images. *arXiv preprint*.

Michael Denkowski and Alon Lavie. 2014. Meteor universal: Language specific translation evaluation for any target language. In *Proceedings of the Ninth Workshop on Statistical Machine Translation*, pages 376–380, Baltimore, Maryland, USA. Association for Computational Linguistics.

Pierre Dognin, Igor Melnyk, Youssef Mroueh, Inkit Padhi, Mattia Rigotti, Jarret Ross, Yair Schiff, Richard A. Young, and Brian Belgodere. 2022. Image captioning as an assistive technology: Lessons learned from vizwiz 2020 challenge. *J. Artif. Int. Res.*, 73.

David Romero et al. 2024a. Cvqa: Culturally-diverse multilingual visual question answering benchmark. *arXiv preprint*.

Gemini Team et al. 2024b. Gemini 1.5: Unlocking multimodal understanding across millions of tokens of context. *arXiv preprint*.

Taraneh Ghandi, Hamidreza Pourreza, and Hamidreza Mahyar. 2023. Deep learning approaches on image captioning: A review. *ACM Comput. Surv.*, 56(3).

Ricardo Gonzalez, Jazmin Collins, Shiri Azenkot, and Cynthia Bennett. 2024. Investigating use cases of ai-powered scene description applications for blind and low vision people. *arXiv preprint*.

Danna Gurari, Qing Li, Abigale J. Stangl, Anhong Guo, Chi Lin, Kristen Grauman, Jiebo Luo, and Jeffrey P. Bigham. 2018. Vizwiz grand challenge: Answering visual questions from blind people. In *2018 IEEE/CVF Conference on Computer Vision and Pattern Recognition*, pages 3608–3617.

Danna Gurari, Yinan Zhao, Meng Zhang, and Nilavra Bhattacharya. 2020. Captioning images taken by people who are blind. In *Computer Vision – ECCV 2020*, pages 417–434, Cham. Springer International Publishing.

Daniel Hershcovich, Stella Frank, Heather Lent, Miryam de Lhoneux, Mostafa Abdou, Stephanie Brandl, Emanuele Bugliarello, Laura Cabello Piqueras, Ilias Chalkidis, Ruixiang Cui, Constanza Fierro, Katerina Margatina, Phillip Rust, and Anders Søgaard. 2022. Challenges and strategies in cross-cultural NLP. In *Proceedings of the 60th Annual Meeting of the Association for Computational Linguistics (Volume 1: Long Papers)*, pages 6997–7013, Dublin, Ireland. Association for Computational Linguistics.

Ziwei Ji, Nayeon Lee, Rita Frieske, Tiezheng Yu, Dan Su, Yan Xu, Etsuko Ishii, Yejin Bang, Andrea Madotto, and Pascale Fung. 2023. Survey of hallucination in natural language generation. *ACM Comput. Surv.*, 55(12):248:1–248:38.

Albert Q. Jiang, Alexandre Sablayrolles, Arthur Mensch, Chris Bamford, Devendra Singh Chaplot, Diego de las Casas, Florian Bressand, Gianna Lengyel, Guillaume Lample, Lucile Saulnier, Lélio Renard Lavaud, Marie-Anne Lachaux, Pierre Stock, Teven Le Scao, Thibaut Lavril, Thomas Wang, Timothée Lacroix, and William El Sayed. 2023. Mistral 7b. *arXiv preprint*.

Ju Yeon Jung, Tom Steinberger, Junbeom Kim, and Mark S. Ackerman. 2022. "so what? what's that to do with me?" expectations of people with visual impairments for image descriptions in their personal photo activities. In *Proceedings of the 2022 ACM Designing Interactive Systems Conference*, DIS '22, page 1893–1906, New York, NY, USA. Association for Computing Machinery.

Hugo Laurençon, Léo Tronchon, Matthieu Cord, and Victor Sanh. 2024. What matters when building vision-language models? *arXiv preprint*.

Junnan Li, Dongxu Li, Silvio Savarese, and Steven C. H. Hoi. 2023a. Blip-2: Bootstrapping language-image pre-training with frozen image encoders and large language models. *arXiv preprint*.

Yifan Li, Yifan Du, Kun Zhou, Jinpeng Wang, Xin Zhao, and Ji-Rong Wen. 2023b. Evaluating object hallucination in large vision-language models. In *Proceedings of the 2023 Conference on Empirical Methods in Natural Language Processing*, pages 292–305, Singapore. Association for Computational Linguistics.

Fangyu Liu, Emanuele Bugliarello, Edoardo Maria Ponti, Siva Reddy, Nigel Collier, and Desmond Elliott. 2021. Visually grounded reasoning across languages and cultures. In *Proceedings of the 2021 Conference on Empirical Methods in Natural Language Processing*, pages 10467–10485, Online and Punta Cana, Dominican Republic. Association for Computational Linguistics.

Haotian Liu, Chunyuan Li, Qingyang Wu, and Yong Jae Lee. 2023a. Visual instruction tuning. In *Advances in Neural Information Processing Systems*, volume 36.

Zhixuan Liu, Youeun Shin, Beverley-Claire Okogwu, Youngsik Yun, Lia Coleman, Peter Schaldenbrand, Jihie Kim, and Jean Oh. 2023b. Towards equitable representation in text-to-image synthesis models with the cross-cultural understanding benchmark (ccub) dataset. *arXiv preprint*.

Oscar Mañas, Pau Rodriguez Lopez, Saba Ahmadi, Aida Nematzadeh, Yash Goyal, and Aishwarya Agrawal. 2023. MAPL: Parameter-efficient adaptation of unimodal pre-trained models for vision-language few-shot prompting. In *Proceedings of the 17th Conference of the European Chapter of the Association for Computational Linguistics*, pages 2523–2548, Dubrovnik, Croatia. Association for Computational Linguistics.

Meredith Ringel Morris, Jazette Johnson, Cynthia L. Bennett, and Edward Cutrell. 2018. Rich representations of visual content for screen reader users. *Proceedings of the 2018 CHI Conference on Human Factors in Computing Systems*.

Anjishnu Mukherjee, Ziwei Zhu, and Antonios Anastasopoulos. 2024. Crossroads of continents: Automated artifact extraction for cultural adaptation with large multimodal models. *arXiv preprint*.

OpenAI. 2024. Hello gpt-4o. blog post.

Kishore Papineni, Salim Roukos, Todd Ward, and Wei-Jing Zhu. 2002. Bleu: a method for automatic evaluation of machine translation. In *Proceedings of the 40th Annual Meeting of the Association for Computational Linguistics*, pages 311–318, Philadelphia, Pennsylvania, USA. Association for Computational Linguistics.

Rita Ramos, Bruno Martins, Desmond Elliott, and Yova Kementchedjhieva. 2023. Smallcap: Lightweight image captioning prompted with retrieval augmentation. In *2023 IEEE/CVF Conference on Computer Vision and Pattern Recognition (CVPR)*, pages 2840–2849.

Anastasia Schaadhardt, Alexis Hiniker, and Jacob O. Wobbrock. 2021. Understanding blind screen-reader users' experiences of digital artboards. In *Proceedings of the 2021 CHI Conference on Human Factors in Computing Systems*, CHI '21, New York, NY, USA. Association for Computing Machinery.

Mrinank Sharma, Meg Tong, Tomasz Korbak, David Duvenaud, Amanda Askell, Samuel R. Bowman, Newton Cheng, Esin Durmus, Zac Hatfield-Dodds, Scott R. Johnston, Shauna Kravec, Timothy Maxwell, Sam McCandlish, Kamal Ndousse, Oliver Rausch, Nicholas Schiefer, Da Yan, Miranda Zhang, and Ethan Perez. 2023. Towards understanding sycophancy in language models. *arXiv preprint*.

Weiyan Shi, Ryan Li, Yutong Zhang, Caleb Ziems, Chunhua yu, Raya Horesh, Rogério Abreu de Paula, and Diyi Yang. 2024. Culturebank: An online community-driven knowledge base towards culturally aware language technologies. *arXiv preprint*.

Ashish V. Thapliyal, Jordi Pont Tuset, Xi Chen, and Radu Soricut. 2022. Crossmodal-3600: A massively multilingual multimodal evaluation dataset. In *Proceedings of the 2022 Conference on Empirical Methods in Natural Language Processing*, pages 715–729, Abu Dhabi, United Arab Emirates. Association for Computational Linguistics.

Ramakrishna Vedantam, C. Lawrence Zitnick, and Devi Parikh. 2015. Cider: Consensus-based image description evaluation. In *2015 IEEE Conference on Computer Vision and Pattern Recognition (CVPR)*, pages 4566–4575.

Mor Ventura, Eyal Ben-David, Anna Korhonen, and Roi Reichart. 2023. Navigating cultural chasms: Exploring and unlocking the cultural pov of text-to-image models. *arXiv preprint*.

Jianfeng Wang, Zhengyuan Yang, Xiaowei Hu, Linjie Li, Kevin Lin, Zhe Gan, Zicheng Liu, Ce Liu, and Lijuan Wang. 2022. GIT: A generative image-to-text transformer for vision and language. *Transactions on Machine Learning Research*.

Thomas Wolf, Lysandre Debut, Victor Sanh, Julien Chaumond, Clement Delangue, Anthony Moi, Pierric Cistac, Tim Rault, Remi Louf, Morgan Funtowicz, Joe Davison, Sam Shleifer, Patrick von Platen, Clara Ma, Yacine Jernite, Julien Plu, Canwen Xu, Teven Le Scao, Sylvain Gugger, Mariama Drame, Quentin Lhoest, and Alexander Rush. 2020. Transformers: State-of-the-art natural language processing. In *Proceedings of the 2020 Conference on Empirical Methods in Natural Language Processing: System Demonstrations*, pages 38–45, Online. Association for Computational Linguistics.

Andre Ye, Sebastin Santy, Jena D. Hwang, Amy X. Zhang, and Ranjay Krishna. 2023. Cultural and linguistic diversity improves visual representations. *arXiv preprint*.

Susan Zhang, Stephen Roller, Naman Goyal, Mikel Artetxe, Moya Chen, Shuohui Chen, Christopher Dewan, Mona Diab, Xian Li, Xi Victoria Lin, Todor Mihaylov, Myle Ott, Sam Shleifer, Kurt Shuster, Daniel Simig, Punit Singh Koura, Anjali Sridhar, Tianlu Wang, and Luke Zettlemoyer. 2022. OPT: Open pre-trained transformer language models. *arXiv preprint*.

A Survey on Caption Preferences

We created a survey aiming to understand the preferences of individuals who seek sighted support regarding image captioning. Our interest was particularly focused on whether they prefer image captions to include cultural information, and how detailed they prefer the descriptions to be. We published our survey through the Prolific platform, by choosing 60 participants with an equal gender sample of and representative across countries compensated with 18$ per hour. We also added a screener and selected participants without corrected/normal vision. Overall, the participants were positive regarding the helpfulness and importance of cultural information in the captions with average ratings of 4.1 and 3.9 respectfully.[5] Participants also tended to prefer short captions compared to longer ones. After the anonymity period, we are going to release our survey link and full results.

B VizWiz Data Filtering—Human Annotation

As mentioned in the experimental set-up section, to filter the data we created a survey through the Prolific annotation platform. All annotators were compensated with 18$ per hour. We ran this survey 4 times asking for 40 participants each time.

We asked people to identify images from the VizWiz dataset based on their cultural background, provide an original and a corrected caption, and specify the reason they selected the image as culture-specific. We grouped the reasons that the annotators provided for selecting culture-specific images in Figure 4.

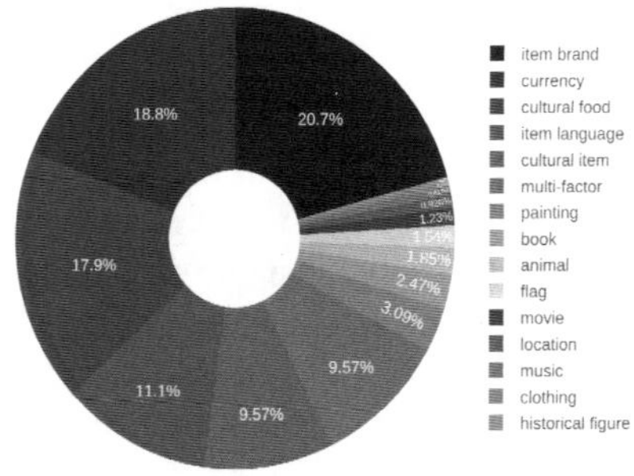

Figure 4: Distribution of the factors/indicators that lead the annotators to select a specific image as culture-related and specify the corresponding culture.

[5]The scale is from 1. Not important/helpful at all to 5. Very important/helpful)

The cultural concepts identified by our annotators can be found in Figure 5.

Figure 5: Distribution of the cultural concepts identified in the VizWiz dataset by the annotators.

The full annotation guidelines were the following:

> Creating datasets that reflect a variety of cultures is a challenging task. This is why we will try to filter an existing dataset. Your task is to find culture-related images from a dataset called VizWiz. You need to:
> - Visit the dataset website[link]. - Browse the dataset or use the search bars on the left side of the page and search key-terms related to your culture 'Within visual question', 'Within visual answer' or 'Within captions'. - Try to find an image that is related to your culture/cultural background (i.e. food brand, currency, books, culture-specific locations etc.) - Provide your answers to the 5 following questions.
>
> 1. Copy and paste the image name (VizWiz_train_**number**.jpg).
> 2. Based on your cultural background, specify what culture you think is the image related to.
> 3. Select a caption for the image from the suggested Image Captions.
> 4. Do you have a better suggestion for the image caption? To guide your caption generation, imagine that you are describing the image to a visually impaired friend. The caption should explain the whole image, including all the main objects, activities, and their relationships, and reflect the culture information of the image.
> 5. Provide a reason as to why the image is culture-specific.

After this, we collected information about the annotators' cultural backgrounds. We asked for both home-country of origin and current country location information since sometimes both can affect our cultural beliefs and practices. The distribution of the annotators counties of origin and location are presented in Figure 6b.

> The last step is to answer some final questions about your cultural background, and age. We do not collect any other personal information. Your answers will only be used for statistical research purposes.
>
> - What is your country of origin that you consider your 'home', influencing your cultural beliefs and other aspects of your identity?
> - Is there a country in which you are currently located for a long period of time?
> - How old are you? Fill in years in numbers.

After collecting all the responses, we kept only the images where at least two annotators agreed to select the image as culture-specific. After this extra validation, we resulted in a total of 324 images spanning 60 different identified cultures. We compared the similarity between the suggested captions by the annotators and the original VizWiz captions and the results can be found in Table 2 indicating a high similarity between the new culture-specific suggested captions.

Captions	BLEU-4	ROUGE-L	F1
Culture-specific	37.10	61.90	93.0

Table 2: Results from comparing the culture-specific captions of the two annotators against the five original VizWiz captions.

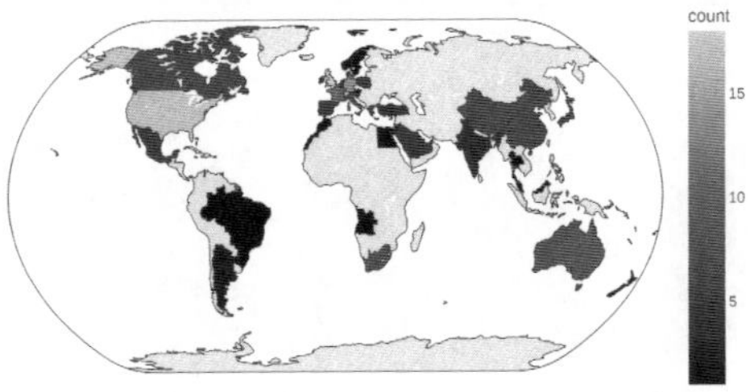

(a) Distribution of the current country location of the annotators.

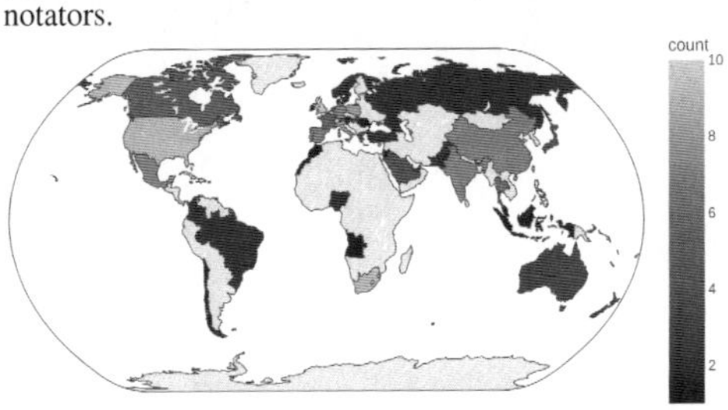

(b) Distribution of the country of origin of the annotators.

Figure 6: Plots as subfigures.

C Model Overview

We list models with their API identifiers in Table 3 below.

Name	Identifier	Reference
BLIP-2	`Salesforce/blip2-opt-6.7b`	Li et al. (2023a)
InstructBLIP	`Salesforce/instructblip-vicuna-7b`	Dai et al. (2023)
Idefics2	`HuggingFaceM4/idefics2-8b`	Laurençon et al. (2024)
LLaVA-1.6	`llava-hf/llava-v1.6-mistral-7b-hf`	Liu et al. (2023a)
Gemini-1.5-Pro	`gemini-1.5-pro-preview-0514`	et al. (2024b)
GPT-4o	`gpt-4o-2024-05-13`	OpenAI (2024)

Table 3: Overview of models used in this study

D Model Prompting

We provide the templates we used to prompt our models. The default templates have been sourced from Dai et al. (2023) and Shi et al. (2024).

E Vizwiz Results – 5 Original References

We report model performance on our filtered VizWiz dataset when using all five original captions per image (rather than combinations of two references at a time) in Figure 5.

F Human Evaluation

To conduct the human evaluation of the model generated responses we created a survey and hired 54 annotators through the Prolific platform compensated with 18$ per hour. We added a screening in the platform for a representative sample of countries and an even distribution of male and female participants. Each annotator evaluated 12 images and their captions and for each image, we assigned two annotators and averaged their scores. We provided the following instructions to the annotators for evaluating the captions:

> This study involves evaluating captions. To guide your ratings, imagine that you are describing the image to a visually impaired friend. Then consider:
> How well does the caption describe the image to this friend? Does it take into account cultural considerations? You will be given two sets of captions describing an image.
>
> 1. Specify which caption you prefer for the given image (1, 2 or both).
> 2. Determine if each caption is accurate and relevant to the given image.
>
> As a general guidance you should consider a caption as bad when it has one or more of the following issues:
> a) Caption misses the main topic of the image. b) Caption has major grammatical errors (such as being incomplete, words in the wrong order, etc). Please ignore the capitalization of words and punctuation. c) Caption includes hallucinations and mentions objects, activities, or relationships that are definitely not in the image. d) Caption is not as informative. e) Caption does not reflect the cultural information depicted in the image.

G Error Analysis II

We provide further examples from currency-related images in Figure 7. We can see that for countries such as US, or Australia, the original VizWiz captions provide culture-specific information, but this is not the case for Japanese or Arabic currencies. Moreover, the models seem robust in western and Asian currencies, but not with all the Arabic ones. The example provided in Figure 7 shows how the models confuse a Jordan currency with Egyptian or Saudi Arabian currencies and how the smaller open-source models are more prone to hallucinations.

Default prompting

```
<Image> A short image description:
```

```
<Image> Write a caption that describes the photo.

Format your response in JSON as follows:
{
  "caption": "Caption for the image"
}
```

```
<Image> A photo of
```

```
<Image> Can you briefly describe the content of the image?
```

```
<Image> Write a caption that describes the photo.
```

Culture-specific prompting

```
<Image> A short, culture-aware image description:
```

```
<Image> Cultural information encompasses content that showcases the distinctive characteristics, artifacts, or manifestations of a
↪ specific group, community, or region.
This includes, but is not limited to, practices, behaviors, norms, values, beliefs, habits, customs, architectural styles,
↪ environmental engagements, and any other elements that are emblematic of a particular cultural setting.
It does not include generic information or widespread practices that are not distinctly tied to a specific cultural identity.

For this task, consider information as "cultural" if:
1. It is associated with or characteristic of a specific identified group (e.g., Americans, Italians, midwestern Americans, etc.).
2. It reveals a unique aspect of that group's way of life, including social conventions, physical creations, or interactions with
↪ their surroundings that are not typically seen in other cultures.
3. It provides insight into the cultural uniqueness, whether through social practices, material culture, or other culturally
↪ significant elements.

Please exclude generic or ubiquitous statements or observations that do not clearly relate to the unique cultural context of a
↪ specific group.

Given this image, do two things:
1. Determine whether the provided example contains cultural information.
2. Write a caption that describes the photo and includes the cultural information extracted.

Format your response in JSON as follows:
{
  "caption": "Caption for the image",
  "is_cultural": true/false,
  "justification": "Why or why not the image contains cultural information"
}
```

```
<Image> Write a caption that describes the photo and includes any cultural information present.
```

Table 4: Image captioning templates used to prompt our models.

H Case Study

We illustrate the value of cultural and inclusive VL models via a case study on evaluating GPT-4V as a visual assistant integrated into the 'Be My Eyes' platform. In this case study, we took a random sample of 20 images from the MaRVL dataset (Liu et al., 2021). Here we provide a selection of images we tried in our case study. Each figure includes the target culture behind each image and the GPT-4 Vision output after loading the image in the Be My Eyes application.

Model	BLEU-4		METEOR		CIDEr		SPICE	
Prompt	*Default*	*Cultural*	*Default*	*Cultural*	*Default*	*Cultural*	*Default*	*Cultural*
Annotation	*Original-Full*		*Original-Full*		*Original-Full*		*Original-Full*	
BLIP-2	<u>14.9</u>	12.1	<u>16.1</u>	15.5	<u>51.7</u>	44.3	<u>10.6</u>	9.9
InstructBLIP	**<u>25.3</u>**	24.5	22.0	<u>22.1</u>	77.4	<u>78.9</u>	<u>15.0</u>	<u>15.0</u>
Idefics2	<u>20.8</u>	16.7	22.2	<u>23.3</u>	**<u>82.0</u>**	76.1	15.1	<u>16.6</u>
LLaVA-1.6	<u>17.3</u>	11.8	<u>23.3</u>	22.1	<u>60.9</u>	40.5	<u>15.3</u>	<u>15.3</u>
Gemini-1.5-Pro	<u>18.6</u>	9.9	<u>25.5</u>	21.9	<u>73.0</u>	15.0	<u>18.0</u>	15.3
GPT-4o	<u>20.5</u>	13.8	**<u>27.4</u>**	24.4	<u>67.7</u>	41.0	**<u>18.4</u>**	16.6

Table 5: Performance of various VLMs on our filtered VizWiz dataset across captioning prompts (default & culture-specific) using the five original reference captions per image. We <u>underline</u> the best result for each model and display the top result for each metric in **bold**.

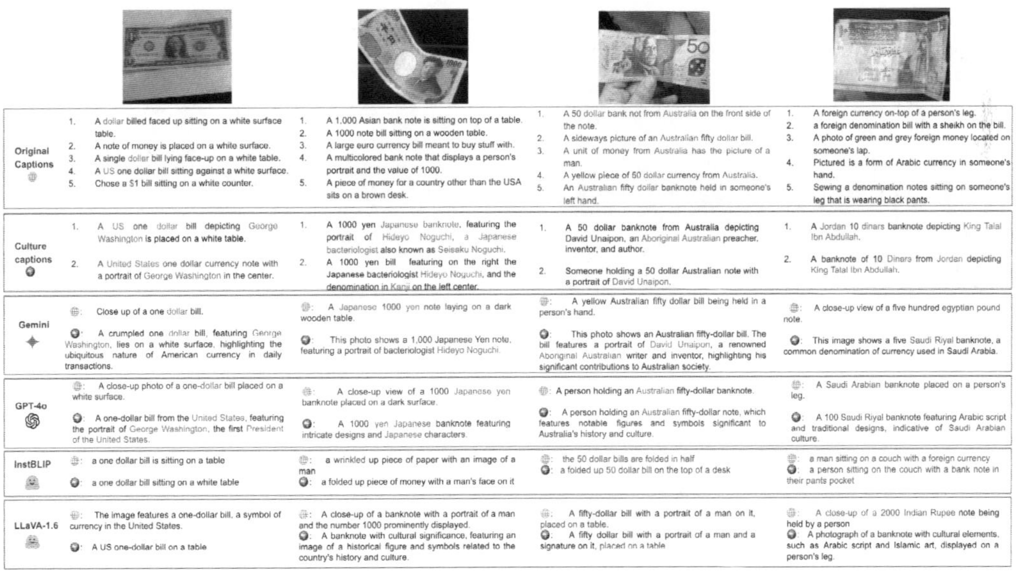

Figure 7: Examples from images related to currency comparing original (🌐) with culture-specific (🌍) annotations and generated captions from Gemini-Pro and GPT-4o with default (🌐) and culture-specific (🌍) prompting.

Figure 8: A picture extracted from MaRVL depicting a statue of Agamas and the GPT-4V image description provided in BeMyEyes.

Figure 9: A picture extracted from MaRVL depicting Buddhist statues and the GPT-4V image description provided in BeMyEyes.

Figure 10: A picture extracted from MaRVL depicting sambar, a traditional Tamil dish, and the GPT-4V image description provided in BeMyEyes.

Figure 11: A picture extracted from MaRVL depicting a döner, a traditional Turkish dish, and the GPT-4V image description provided in BeMyEyes.

Evaluating Large Language Models on Social Signal Sensitivity: An Appraisal Theory Approach

Zhen Wu, Ritam Dutt, Carolyn Penstein Rosé

Language Technologies Institute, Carnegie Mellon University
{zhenwu,rdutt,cprose}@cs.cmu.edu

Abstract

We present a framework to assess the sensitivity of Large Language Models (LLMs) to textually embedded social signals using an Appraisal Theory perspective. We report on an experiment that uses prompts encoding three dimensions of social signals: Affect, Judgment, and Appreciation. In response to the prompt, an LLM generates both an analysis (Insight) and a conversational Response, which are analyzed in terms of sensitivity to the signals. We quantitatively evaluate the output text through topical analysis of the Insight and predicting the social intelligence scores of the Response in terms of empathy and emotional polarity. Key findings show that LLMs are more sensitive to positive signals. The personas impact Responses but not the Insight. We discuss how our framework can be extended to a broader set of social signals, personas, and scenarios to evaluate LLM behaviors under various conditions.

1 Introduction

"The limits of my language mean the limits of my world." (Wittgenstein, 1922)

The increasing integration of Large Language Models (LLMs) into social contexts presents a critical challenge: How effectively can they process and respond to social signals embedded in human language? Social signals, as defined in Poggi and Francesca (2010), are communicative or informative signals that convey insights into social actions (e.g., insulting someone), interactions (e.g., showing responsiveness), emotions (e.g., reflecting joy), attitudes (e.g., exhibiting disgust), and relationships (e.g., showing closeness). These social signals are tools in interaction for maintaining or changing relationships that set the stage for effective human-human interactions, which may shape the responses of LLMs when they engage as participants in hybrid settings involving both humans and LLMs.

This paper illustrates a methodology for systematic investigation of the sensitivity of LLMs to social signals in role-playing scenarios. In particular, the research specifically focuses on social signals grounded in Appraisal Theory (Martin and White, 2005) — Affect, Judgment, and Appreciation. These dimensions facilitate a nuanced understanding of how human language expresses emotions, makes ethical judgments, and appreciates the significance of practices respectively. In particular, the research aims to address two main questions:

- **RQ1:** How sensitive are current LLMs to the variations of social signals embedded in language, both in terms of ability to explain the encoding of social signals in the text and to respond in ways that exhibit the response the signal is meant to elicit?
- **RQ2:** From a more nuanced perspective related to generality across contexts, when an LLM is provided with a persona to influence response generation, how and to what extent do different personas affect the sensitivity of LLMs to Appraisal-based social signals?

The research paradigm is displayed in Figure 1. The framework is meant to assess specific capabilities of LLMs, identify limitations, and address challenges in utilizing socio-linguistic theories in such evaluations. Our contributions are as follows:

- We take an exploratory approach to investigate the sensitivity of LLMs to social signals grounded in Appraisal Theory (Martin and White, 2005).
- Our experimental design is systematically controlled and can be generalized to a broader set of social signals and language framing, personas, and social scenarios to evaluate the elicited behaviors of LLMs under diverse and complex conditions.

Proceedings of the 1st Human-Centered Large Language Modeling Workshop, pages 67–80

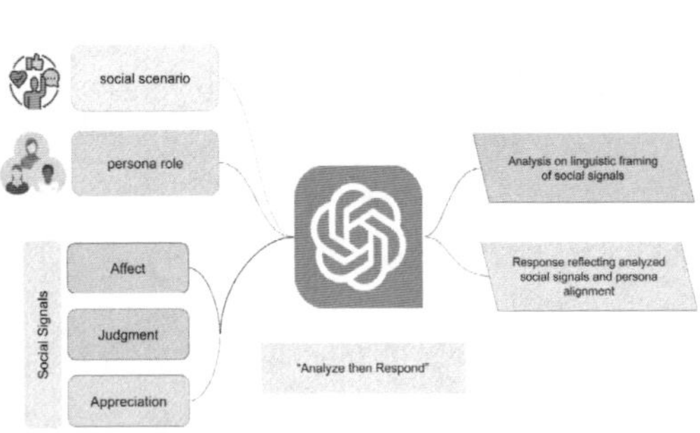

Figure 1: An overview of our evaluative framework assessing the sensitivity of LLMs to social signals (Affect, Judgment, Appreciation) based on Appraisal Theory.

- Our findings reveal the limited sensitivity of LLMs to negative aspects of social signals.

We make our code and data publicly available below. [1]

2 Related Work

From a technical perspective, this paper investigates the specific capabilities of LLMs to operate in contextually appropriate ways in different social settings. From a linguistic perspective, we are specifically interested in Appraisal Theory (Martin and White, 2005) to define a space of social signals because of its prevalence in the field of language technologies. Thus, we review past work from both a technical and linguistic perspective.

2.1 Role of LLMs in Social Interactions

Recently LLMs have seen use in enactment and analysis of social interactions, such as multi-agent communication (Chan et al., 2023; Li et al., 2023), social robotics (Addlesee et al., 2024; Hanschmann et al., 2024), simulation of human-like interactions within complex social systems (Zhou et al., 2024; Xie et al., 2024), and identification of implicit meaning and conversations dynamics (Dutt et al., 2024; Hua et al., 2024). However, challenges in accurately simulating and understanding complex social dynamics persist. For instance, past work on social signal detection with LLMs has revealed that LLMs only exhibit moderate success at best, and especially struggle with signals that involve more nuanced understanding of language, such as trustworthiness and offensiveness (Choi et al., 2023).

The term social signals is multifaceted and encompasses a broad range of meanings. Our work extends past research by focusing on 3 specific dimensions of social signals defined in Appraisal theory (Martin and White, 2005). Our investigation employs an experimental approach grounded in the vignette study paradigm (Converse et al., 2015; Veloski et al., 2005; Sheringham et al., 2021). Moreover, we explore different variations and combinations of social signals in order to push the limits of sensitivity and separatability as we examine the variation in LLM-generated outputs as we manipulate the input. Such a setting can facilitate understanding of how LLMs process and respond to language where multiple strategies are at play simultaneously, as is often the case in human-human interaction.

2.2 Appraisal Theory in Language Analysis

The Appraisal Theory of Martin and White (2005) provides a framework for analyzing how language expresses emotions, attitudes, and stances by means of linguistic choices, thereby influencing interpersonal communication and relationship formation and maintenance. Initially, the theory was utilized in NLP to enhance sentiment classification (Whitelaw et al., 2005). Later, Kenneth et al. (2007) and Khoo et al. (2012) extended it to broader contexts such as analysis of news opinion and online news articles, highlighting its utility in media analysis. Further, Howley et al. (2013) explored the theory within the context of small group communication, analyzing how linguistic patterns influenced group dynamics and decision-making processes. Our work is unique in that it links model performance on detection and explanation of social signals with work on generating a response to social signals.

More recently, Imamovic et al. (2024) used ChatGPT to annotate attitudes and emotions in text based on Appraisal Theory. They addressed challenges in achieving consistent and accurate annotations. While the model demonstrated high precision in recognizing the Appraisal expressions, it showed low recall and struggled in accurately assigning these expressions to correct categories. Similarly, our work aims to further evaluate the interpretive skills of LLMs within a sociolinguistic frame of reference and to enhance our understanding of how these models process combinations of nuanced social signals in interpersonal scenarios.

[1] https://github.com/zhenwu0831/LLM_social-signal_sensitivity

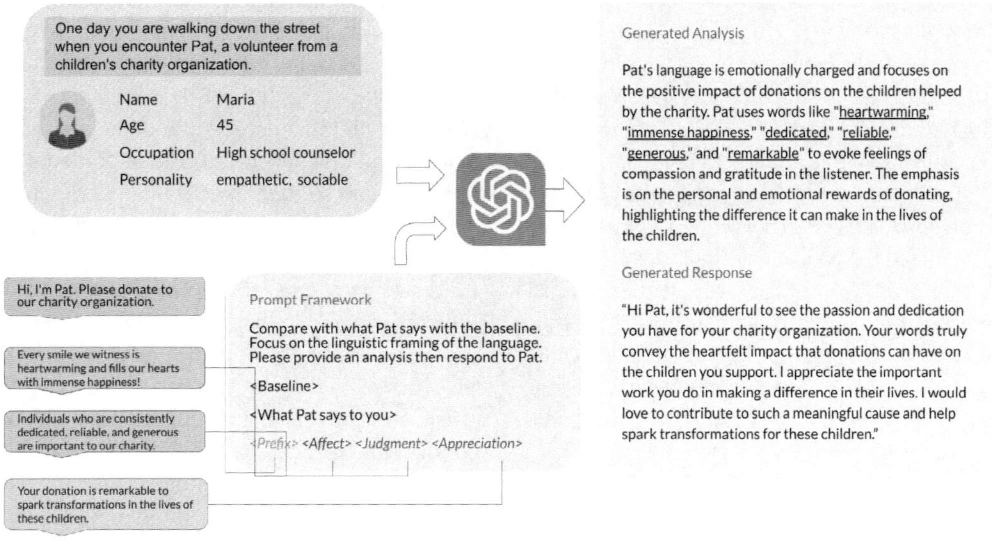

Figure 2: Here we illustrate one example of input and output of our evaluative framework. We employ the "Persuasion for Good" social scenario and create personas with their Name, Age, Occupation, and Personality (blue box on the top). In the prompt (gray box at the bottom), we include our well-crafted utterance, structured according to a predefined template to incorporate the three social signals: Affect, Judgment, Appreciation. The model subsequently generates an analysis on the utterance and provides a direct response (yellow box on the right).

Signal	Polarity	Example Utterance
AF	Positive	"Seeing the community come together in such a wonderful way gives us hope!"
	Negative	"It's truly miserable to witness the pain and suffering of these innocent lives."
JG	Positive	"People who are selfless and generous are the backbone of our charity community."
	Negative	"Some people are not generous, often holding back support when it's most needed."
AP	Positive	" Your donation will provide essential support and care for lives of countless children."
	Negative	"Without your donation, our actions become less effective and do not reach potential."

Table 1: Example utterances of positive and negative polarity for the different kinds of social signals corresponding to Affect (AF), Judgment (JG), and Appreciation (AP).

3 Method

3.1 Experimental Paradigm: Vignette Study

Because our aim is to systematically investigate how the behavior of an LLM changes in response to embedded social signals, we employ a vignette design similar to prior work (Converse et al., 2015; Veloski et al., 2005; Sheringham et al., 2021). Typically, in a vignette study a text describes a persona, a scenario, and an event, and a participant (in our case, an LLM) performs some role-playing task in response to that setting. It is used as a form of simulation study. In particular, an experimentally manipulated text serves as a prompt to an LLM (GPT-3.5-turbo, GPT-4-turbo), and the properties of the generated output (response) are measured. The prompt encodes a persona in a task setting for the LLM, and an input utterance with social signals embedded in it. The LLM is asked to provide an analysis of the text (which we refer to as Insight) from the standpoint of language framing as well as the response to the text as the persona. The extent of the interaction per prompt is just one conversational exchange. Specifically, we adapt the Persuasion for Good (Wang et al., 2019) scenario where the user enacts the role of Pat, a volunteer for a charity organization to persuade the LLM, which enacts a predefined persona, to donate to the charity.

In our study, we focus on the *Attitudes* component of the Appraisal framework (Martin and White, 2005), which itself can be further subdivided into three general types: *Affect* (a conveyed emotional state), *Judgment* (ethics and moral assessments of dependability), and *Appreciation* (values of practices). For simplicity and inspired by the original Martin and White's book of Appraisal Theory (Martin and White, 2005), each social signal — Affect (AF), Judgment (JG), and Appreciation (AP) — is categorized into two polarities, i.e., positive or negative based on specific words that are associated with the signal. We present words that exemplify each category in Table 2 and pair those sets with hand crafted utterances that capture the polarities in the social signals. These manipulated texts are then used as input for our LLM. Using these manipulated texts, we are able to experimentally vary the value of each social signal (i.e., positive or negative) in order to test for measured changes in the LLM responses resulting from that experimental manipulation of social signals.

In our experiment, we designed three different personas with diverse personalities to see how those differences would influence different behaviors in response to social signals. The diversity is with respect to the OCEAN values (Openness, Conscientiousness, Extraversion, Agreeableness, and Neuroticism) from the Big-Five personality framework (Goldberg, 1992). We demonstrate the OCEAN values of our personas in Table 6. The three personas include an empathetic and sociable high school counselor, an ambitious and assertive tech entrepreneur (leader), and an adventurous and creative artist. We prompt the same input utterances for all three personas.

Our primary objectives are 1) to enable the behaviors of LLMs to systematically vary in response to each social signal that serves as an independent variable (AF, JG, AP); 2) to ensure that the LLMs' responses consistently reflect these behavioral changes across different personas; 3) to accurately measure the behavioral differences. To achieve these goals, we meticulously craft input utterances to isolate and control each social signal (Section 3.2), design an "Analyze then Respond" prompt to generate insights and responses to these signal-imbued utterances (Section 3.3), and establish measurements to quantify properties of LLM responses (Section 3.4). An overview of our vignette study is illustrated in Figure 2.

3.2 Signal-Embedded Utterance Creation

To systematically assess the impact of individual social signals on the LLMs' generation, we create short utterances that each encapsulate a single, distinct social signal, which then subsequently serve as building blocks for more complex text. For each type (positive or negative) of social signal (AF, JG, AP), we craft 5 distinct short utterances with the same length. These 5 utterances are phrased differently but are signal-wise identical. For example, both the utterances *"Your donation will help develop safe environments where children can learn and grow."* and *"Even your smallest donation will support a child with food, education, and healthcare."* express the positive outcomes of donations thus reflecting AP-positive, although their wording differs. We provide example utterances for each type of signal in Table 1.

We design a template to systematically control and integrate the three social signals into a more extensive text. The template is structured as follows: `<Prefix>` `<Affect>` `<Judgment>` `<Appreciation>`. The prefix is a standard, neutral introduction statement: "Hi, I'm Pat. Please donate to our charity organization." It establishes some prior conversational context, ensuring that the subsequent social signal feels coherent. Following this prefix, we append short sentences that each represent one social signal among AF, JG, and AP, along with their corresponding polarity (positive or negative). This structure allows us to systematically manipulate each dimension of social signals independently while maintaining control over the context and content of the interaction.

For our controlled investigation, the complete set of stimuli is generated through a full factorial design spanning across Persona (i.e., counselor, artist, and leader), social signals (i.e., AF, JG, AP), and polarity of each signal signal (i.e., positive or negative). Furthermore, for each social signal of a given polarity, we generate five utterances corresponding to that type. Consequently, over 24 possible unique settings, our dataset comprises 1000 unique utterances, which are used for subsequent analysis.

3.3 "Analyze then Respond" Prompt

We design an "Analyze then Respond" prompt to instruct the models to generate analysis and responses to nuanced social signals from the experimental manipulation (Figure 3). In order to facilitate the linguistic analysis of the input utterance, we also craft a neutral utterance for the LLM to compare it to. In that neutral utterance, each social signal has a neutral polarity and serves as a control. We posit that this design will help us distinctly measure the

```
[System message]

Pretend you are {Persona}. One day you are walking down the street when
you encounter Pat, a volunteer from a children's charity organization.

Compare with what Pat says with the neutral utterance. Focus on the
linguistic framing of the language. Please provide an analysis then
respond to Pat.


[User message]

<Neutral utterance>
Hi, I'm Pat. Please donate to our charity organization. It's another day
at the charity, and we continue our work as usual. Involvement levels in
our charity organization frequently vary from one individual to another.
Every donation will be allocated according to our ongoing programs and
current goals.

<What Pat says to you>
{signal-embedded utterance}
```

Figure 3: Our "Analyze then Respond" prompt. In the system message, we provide the persona and scenario information. In user message, we present a neutral utterance and ask the model to perform a comparative analysis between the neutral utterance and the signal-embedded utterance, with a focus on linguistic framing. Following this, we instruct the model to directly respond to the signal-embedded utterance.

impact of varied social signals. We use the same neutral utterance while prompting with different signal-embedded utterances.

We prompt the LLMs with the persona, social scenario, neutral utterance, and our controlled utterances that incorporate specific social signals. Each prompt requires the LLMs to engage in two tasks: 1) **Analysis**: The LLMs must first generate an analysis of the linguistic framing of the signal-embedded utterance in comparison to the neutral utterance. This involves addressing changes along the three signals and their potential impact on the message conveyed in the signal-embedded utterance. We refer to this analysis subsequently as an "**Insight**". 2) **Response**: Following the generated Insight, the LLMs are also required to output a response to the signal-embedded utterance. Ideally, the response should be contextually appropriate and sensitive to social signal variations in the input utterance, and align with the instructed persona.

Our empirical evidence suggests that when the models are instructed to compare the input utterance with a neutral utterance before producing the Response, their generated Responses contain more persona-related details and exhibit a more engaged tone. We demonstrate one example comparing the Response generated by GPT-3.5 with and without this analysis step in Figure 4.

3.4 Measurement of Behavioral Changes

We carry out two different kinds of analysis to quantify the impact of the experimental manipulation on the generated outputs of LLMs. The differentiation is motivated by addressing the unique requirements of each phase in our evaluation framework.

For the generated Insight, our objective is to assess whether the specific words that exemplify each social signal are present. Thus, we quantify Insight through a topical modelling approach, the details of which appear in Section 3.4.1.

On the other hand, for the generated Response, our goal is to measure how the Response changes as we manipulate the input social signals. Therefore, we assess the Response along the dimensions of social intelligence described in Section 3.4.2.

Signal	Polarity	Seed words
AF	Positive	cheerful, buoyant, love
	Negative	sad, miserable, heartbroken
JG	Positive	reliable, dependable, resolute
	Negative	unreliable, weak, unfaithful
AP	Positive	valuable, helpful, exceptional
	Negative	insignificant, ineffective, useless

Table 2: Seed words to Affect (AF), Judgment (JG), and Appreciation (AP).

3.4.1 Topical Modelling of Insight

To analyse the generated Insight, we employ the Stanford Empath tool (Fast et al., 2016) as our tool of choice for topic modelling. Empath facilitates text analysis by counting the occurrences of words that belong to predefined or user-defined lexical categories. From a set of seed words, Empath creates new user-defined categories by identifying semantically related words through its embeddings trained on an extensive corpus.

We define specific lexical categories within Empath to correspond to the different polarities (positive or negative) of social signals (Affect, Judgment, and Appreciation). These categories are constructed using seed words carefully chosen to exemplify each signal, as previously illustrated in the examples (see Table 2). We create 5 categories that have a logical connection with the encoding of Appraisal social signals in the input. These include *Optimism* which includes both the positive and negative dimension of Affect (AF), *Admire* and *Criticise* to account for the positive and negative polarity of the Judgment signal (JG) respectively, and the *Worthwhile* and *Negligible* categories for positive and negative Appreciation (AP) respectively . We consolidate the positive and negative polarity of AF into a single category of "Optimism" because AF directly influences the overall emotional tone, either enhancing Optimism or decreasing it. This is different from JG and AP, which require distinct categories to capture their specific nuances. Each category is enriched with related words identified by Empath, resulting in a lexicon consisting of 100 words for each category.

We anticipate that the effect of each input social signal (AF, JG, AP) should be most distinct in their corresponding Empath categories. For example, positive and negative signals of AF should prominently influence the "Optimism" category, while signals related to JG should be correlated more with the "Admire" and "Criticise" categories. Moreover, this pattern of results should be consistent across different personas. However, we also expect that the magnitude of these effects may vary based on the specific persona. For instance, an empathetic persona (the counselor) may exhibit stronger responses to positive social signals compared to a more assertive tech entrepreneur persona (the leader).

3.4.2 Measuring Social Intelligence of Response

In addition to the predefined topical categories curated from Empath, we also measure the association of the generated Response corresponding to the intensity and polarity of emotions and empathy, which we subsume under the umbrella term of "social intelligence".

To this end, we use the Empathic Conversations dataset (Omitaomu et al., 2022), designed to analyse emotional and empathetic responses in dialogues. It comprises dialogues where participants discuss news articles and each conversational turn is annotated for the level of expressed empathy, emotional polarity, and emotional intensity.

These three dimensions of social intelligence are formulated from a third-party perspective where emotional polarity refers to whether the utterance is negative, neutral, or positive (from a range of 1 to 3), while emotional intensity and empathy are coded on an ordinal scale from 1 to 5, with one being the lowest for both cases. This dataset was employed for the shared task of predicting different dimensions of social intelligence at ACL 2023 and 2024 (Barriere et al., 2023).

Based on the findings on the shared task, we fine-tune the base-variant of the DeBERTa model (He et al., 2021) on the train split for all three tasks. Our model achieves a moderate Pearson's correlation coefficient on the development split of the dataset with a score of 0.76, 0.63, and 0.67 for the three tasks of emotional polarity, emotional intensity, and empathy respectively. To conform with our current vignette setting, where the conversation is limited to one turn of conversational exchange, we use only the previous turn as context for determining the social intelligence scores.

We thus quantify the Response generated by the LLMs in accordance with these dimensions of emotional polarity, emotional intensity, and empathy. We describe the details of our analysis in the following section.

4 Results and Discussions

With the quantitative metrics of Insight and Response established (Empath categories and social intelligence scores), we proceed to conduct a statistical analysis of our experimental results.

At the outset, we want to ensure that the quantitative metrics chosen are indeed separable from each other, i.e., there are no associations between them.

Thus, we conduct a factor analysis with varimax rotation, a statistical method to identify distinct, principle factors from the quantitative metrics of Insight and Response. If the quantitative metrics are loaded onto separate factors without overlapping, then the metrics are deemed as separable. We refer to the separable quantitative metrics as "Factors".

Following this, we subsequently conduct an ANOVA (Analysis of Variance), a statistical method that evaluates which input variables (social signals, personas, and types of LLMs) significantly influence the Factors and to what extent. We define the independent variables of ANOVA as 3 personas, 3 social signals, 2 types of LLMs, and the Factors, while the dependent variables are the scores of the Factors. To further investigate the interactions between the variables, we also include both pairwise interaction terms between the independent variables (persona-signal, signal-model, signal-Factors, model-Factors) and the 3-way interaction terms between model, Factors, and social signals. Due to space constraints, we have included the detailed results corresponding to both the Insight and Response in Appendix Section 7.1 and Section 7.2. Below we provide a summary of the salient results.

4.1 Results Pertaining to the Insight

We assess how the different Empath categories, i.e., — Optimism, Admire, Criticise, Worthwhile, and Negligible — are processed by GPT-3.5 and GPT-4. The factor analysis reveals that each Empath category forms a distinct factor, with each category's scores loading strongly onto a separate factor ($\approx .71$). This indicates that the Insights generated by GPT-3.5 can be clearly distinguished across these categories. In contrast, the factor analysis of GPT-4 Insights shows some overlap, particularly with the Negligible category loading onto both the Worthwhile category and another separate factor. This overlap suggests that the Insights generated by GPT-4 are not well-separable with respect to the Worthwhile category. To maintain clarity and avoid potential misinterpretation of results caused by this overlap, we exclude Worthwhile from further analysis of the generated Insight. Consequently, our Insight Factors include Optimism, Admire, Criticise, and Negligible.

In our subsequent ANOVA, we use Personas, Affect (AF), Judgment (JG), Appreciation (AP), Model type (GPT-3.5, GPT-4), and Insight Factors as independent variables, with the quantitative values of these Insight Factors serving as the dependent variables. Our ANOVA model explains 59% of the variance in the dependent variables. The ANOVA results indicate that both models exhibit statistically significant sensitivity to the social signals (AF, JG, AP) embedded within the input utterances ($p < .0001$). This finding suggests that the generated Insights from both models generally address keywords associated with each social signal accurately. Notably, it aligns well with our expectations that the effects of these social signals are most prominent in their corresponding Empath categories. Post-hoc analysis using Student's t-test reveals that positive Affect corresponds to an increase in the "Optimism" category, and positive Judgment is associated with higher scores for "Admire" and vice versa for the "Criticise" category. Additionally, positive Appreciation corresponds to decreased "Negligible" scores.

We showcase the mean and the standard deviation of the scores for these corresponding Empath categories in Table 3. The low value of the scores can be explained by the fact that Empath normalizes the scores over the length of each generated Insight sentence. Our table also highlights the more pronounced results for the Insight for GPT-3.5 than GPT-4. Based on this, we also calculate Cohen's d effect sizes to further quantify the magnitude of the statistical significant sensitivity, by measuring the differences between positive and negative groups for each social signal, each Empath category and each model. We similarly find that the effect size is most prominent for each social signal in its corresponding Empath categories. We present the values of Cohen's d that indicate large effect sizes in Table 7.

4.2 Results Pertaining to the Response

We investigate how the different social intelligence dimensions, i.e., — Empathy, Emotional Intensity, and Emotional Polarity — and Empath categories are processed by GPT-3.5 and GPT-4. In the factor analysis, for GPT-3.5, the separation into factors is clean, with four out of five factors showing very strong associations (loadings of at least 0.9) with the output metrics (social intelligence dimensions and Empath categories). Each output metric is primarily associated with one specific factor (loading above 0.3). In contrast, GPT-4 shows greater overlap between factors, suggesting a less distinct separation of its Response with respect to each output

LLM	Empath	Affect Positive	Affect Negative	Judgment Positive	Judgment Negative	Appreciation Positive	Appreciation Negative	Persona Counselor	Persona Artist	Persona Leader
GPT3.5	optimism	**0.05±0.02**	0.01±0.01	0.03±0.03	0.03±0.03	0.03±0.03	0.03±0.03	0.03±0.03	0.03±0.03	0.03±0.02
GPT3.5	admire	0.01±0.01	0.01±0.01	**0.02±0.01**	0.01±0.01	0.01±0.01	0.01±0.01	0.01±0.01	0.01±0.01	0.01±0.01
GPT3.5	criticise	0.01±0.01	0.01±0.01	0.0±0.0	**0.02±0.02**	0.01±0.01	0.01±0.01	0.01±0.01	0.01±0.01	0.01±0.01
GPT3.5	worthwhile	0.01±0.01	0.01±0.01	0.01±0.02	0.01±0.01	**0.02±0.02**	0.01±0.01	0.01±0.02	0.01±0.01	0.01±0.01
GPT3.5	negligible	0.0±0.01	0.01±0.01	0.0±0.01	0.01±0.01	0.0±0.0	0.01±0.01	0.01±0.01	0.01±0.01	0.01±0.01
GPT4	optimism	**0.04±0.02**	0.02±0.01	0.03±0.02	0.03±0.02	0.03±0.02	0.03±0.02	0.03±0.02	0.03±0.02	0.03±0.02
GPT4	admire	0.01±0.01	0.01±0.01	**0.02±0.01**	0.01±0.01	0.01±0.01	0.01±0.01	0.01±0.01	0.01±0.01	0.01±0.01
GPT4	criticise	0.01±0.01	0.01±0.01	0.0±0.0	0.01±0.01	0.01±0.01	0.01±0.01	0.01±0.01	0.01±0.01	0.01±0.01
GPT4	worthwhile	0.02±0.01	0.02±0.01	0.02±0.01	0.02±0.01	0.02±0.01	0.01±0.01	0.02±0.01	0.02±0.01	0.02±0.01
GPT4	negligible	0.01±0.01	0.01±0.01	0.01±0.01	0.01±0.01	0.0±0.0	0.01±0.0	0.01±0.01	0.01±0.01	0.01±0.01

Table 3: We present the mean and standard deviation of the five categories of Empath topic (Optimism, Admire, Criticise, Worthwhile, Negligible) for the generated LLMs' Insight. The highest values are boldfaced.

LLM	Categories	Affect Positive	Affect Negative	Judgment Positive	Judgment Negative	Appreciation Positive	Appreciation Negative	Persona Counselor	Persona Artist	Persona Leader
GPT3.5	Emo Pol	0.12±0.09	0.22±0.16	0.16±0.13	0.18±0.15	0.16±0.13	0.18±0.15	0.13±0.13	0.21±0.15	0.17±0.12
GPT3.5	Emo Int	2.73±0.34	2.71±0.35	2.75±0.34	2.69±0.35	2.77±0.33	2.68±0.36	2.92±0.3	2.61±0.39	2.63±0.23
GPT3.5	Empathy	3.15±0.14	3.29±0.13	3.23±0.15	3.22±0.15	3.24±0.15	3.20±0.15	3.28±0.13	3.24±0.16	3.15±0.14
GPT4	Emo Pol	0.14±0.07	0.26±0.17	0.19±0.14	0.20±0.15	0.19±0.13	0.21±0.15	0.26±0.18	0.16±0.12	0.18±0.09
GPT4	Emo Int	2.54±0.27	2.57±0.29	2.59±0.28	2.51±0.27	2.57±0.28	2.54±0.27	2.58±0.28	2.67±0.27	2.42±0.22
GPT4	Empathy	3.13±0.15	3.3±0.13	3.23±0.15	3.19±0.17	3.23±0.16	3.19±0.17	3.25±0.14	3.28±0.13	3.11±0.16

Table 4: Mean and standard deviation of scores corresponding to social intelligence i.e emotional polarity (Emo Pol), emotional intensity (Emo Int), and Empathy for the Response.

metric. Based on these findings, we focus our subsequent analysis on 5 principal Response Factors — Emotional Intensity, Emotional Polarity/Optimism (Negative Affect), Empathy, Admire, and Criticise — while excluding others like "Worthwhile" and "Negligible" due to their overlapping factor loadings.

We carry out a similar ANOVA analysis as we do for the Insight, where we use Persona, AF, JG, and AP signals, the Model type (GPT3.5, GPT4), and Response Factors as the independent variables, with the quantitative values of these 5 principle Response Factors as the dependent variables. This ANOVA model explains 99% of the variance in the dependent variables. We present the statistics of the three dimensions of social intelligence in Table 4. Our key findings from the ANOVA include:

Sensitivity to social signals across all Factors Similarly to the results regarding the Insight, the models' Responses are statistically significant ($p < .0001$) to the social signals, indicating that both LLMs, in general, can effectively respond to various social signals in language. Based on a student-t posthoc analysis, we synthesize the specific patterns in the following paragraphs.

Distinctive impact of negative Affect Both models exhibit significant sensitivity to negative Affect, particularly enhancing empathy and emotional polarity scores. However, the impact of negative Affect on emotional intensity varies between the models: Response of GPT-3.5 shows an increase, whereas GPT-4 Response demonstrates a decrease. This different response pattern provides insights into how these models might be applied to elicit desired behaviors: GPT-3.5's increase in intensity might make it more suitable for scenarios requiring strong, clear emotional displays, while GPT-4's decrease in intensity could make it better suited for contexts where a more measured or controlled response is preferable.

Limited sensitivity to negative social evaluations Both models' Responses show increased empathy and emotional intensity in relation to positive Judgment and Appreciation signals, while displaying limited or non-significant sensitivity to negative aspects of these signals. This tendency to respond strongly to positive evaluations suggests a potential overemphasis that might skew the models' responses, addressing their limited performance in scenarios involving mixed or negative feedback.

Robust and consistent patterns across personas We have found that the interactions between personas and other variables are not significant or even marginal. This indicates that the aforementioned response patterns are consistent across different personas. However, we have also observed that different personas exhibit various levels of social intelligence in the generated Response. For example, the ambitious and assertive leader persona has a consistently lower empathy score than that of the counselor or artist for both models.

5 Conclusion

In this study, we design a systematic framework to evaluate the sensitivity of GPT-3.5 and GPT-4 to key social signals based on Appraisal Theory, i.e. Affect, Judgment, and Appreciation. The results confirm that these models demonstrate statistically significant sensitivity to the three social signals. However, our findings also uncover their limited sensitivity to negative aspects of social signals. Future research could extend these findings by including a wider range of LLMs and exploring additional output measures to enhance our understanding of LLMs' capabilities in social contexts. Through this work, we provide a generalizable framework that can be extended to a broader set of social signals and language framing beyond Appraisal Theory, as well as various social scenarios and personas, thus systematically evaluating the elicited behaviors of LLMs under diverse and complex conditions.

6 Limitations

Focus on GPT Family Models Our study mainly focuses on the GPT family models, GPT-3.5 and GPT-4. Future research should include a broader range of LLMs to determine if the observed patterns of sensitivity to social signals are consistent across different LLMs.

Selective Output Measures We use specific measures such as Empath categories and empathy- and emotional-related metrics. While these measures have provided valuable insights, expanding the range of output measures in future studies could offer a more comprehensive view of the models' capabilities.

References

Angus Addlesee, Neeraj Cherakara, Nivan Nelson, Daniel Hernández García, Nancie Gunson, Weronika Sieińska, Marta Romeo, Christian Dondrup, and Oliver Lemon. 2024. A multi-party conversational social robot using llms. In *Companion of the 2024 ACM/IEEE International Conference on Human-Robot Interaction*, HRI '24, page 1273–1275, New York, NY, USA. Association for Computing Machinery.

Valentin Barriere, João Sedoc, Shabnam Tafreshi, and Salvatore Giorgi. 2023. Findings of WASSA 2023 shared task on empathy, emotion and personality detection in conversation and reactions to news articles. In *Proceedings of the 13th Workshop on Computational Approaches to Subjectivity, Sentiment, & Social Media Analysis*, pages 511–525, Toronto, Canada. Association for Computational Linguistics.

Chi-Min Chan, Weize Chen, Yusheng Su, Jianxuan Yu, Wei Xue, Shanghang Zhang, Jie Fu, and Zhiyuan Liu. 2023. Chateval: Towards better llm-based evaluators through multi-agent debate. *Preprint*, arXiv:2308.07201.

Minje Choi, Jiaxin Pei, Sagar Kumar, Chang Shu, and David Jurgens. 2023. Do LLMs understand social knowledge? evaluating the sociability of large language models with SocKET benchmark. In *Proceedings of the 2023 Conference on Empirical Methods in Natural Language Processing*, pages 11370–11403, Singapore. Association for Computational Linguistics.

Lara Converse, Kirsten Barrett, Eugene Rich, and James Reschovsky. 2015. Methods of observing variations in physicians' decisions: The opportunities of clinical vignettes. *Journal of General Internal Medicine*, 30(S3):586–594.

Ritam Dutt, Zhen Wu, Kelly Shi, Divyanshu Sheth, Prakhar Gupta, and Carolyn Penstein Rose. 2024. Leveraging machine-generated rationales to facilitate social meaning detection in conversations. *Preprint*, arXiv:2406.19545.

Ethan Fast, Binbin Chen, and Michael S Bernstein. 2016. Empath: Understanding topic signals in large-scale text. In *Proceedings of the 2016 CHI conference on human factors in computing systems*, pages 4647–4657.

Lewis R Goldberg. 1992. The development of markers for the big-five factor structure. *Psychological assessment*, 4(1):26.

Leon Hanschmann, Ulrich Gnewuch, and Alexander Maedche. 2024. Saleshat: A llm-based social robot for human-like sales conversations. In *Chatbot Research and Design*, pages 61–76, Cham. Springer Nature Switzerland.

Pengcheng He, Xiaodong Liu, Jianfeng Gao, and Weizhu Chen. 2021. Deberta: Decoding-enhanced bert with disentangled attention. In *International Conference on Learning Representations*.

Iris K. Howley, Elijah Mayfield, and Carolyn Penstein Rosé. 2013. Linguistic analysis methods for studying small groups.

Yilun Hua, Nicholas Chernogor, Yuzhe Gu, Seoyeon Jeong, Miranda Luo, and Cristian Danescu-Niculescu-Mizil. 2024. How did we get here? summarizing conversation dynamics. In *Proceedings of the 2024 Conference of the North American Chapter of the Association for Computational Linguistics: Human Language Technologies (Volume 1: Long Papers)*, pages 7452–7477, Mexico City, Mexico. Association for Computational Linguistics.

Mirela Imamovic, Silvana Deilen, Dylan Glynn, and Ekaterina Lapshinova-Koltunski. 2024. Using ChatGPT for annotation of attitude within the appraisal theory: Lessons learned. In *Proceedings of The 18th Linguistic Annotation Workshop (LAW-XVIII)*, pages 112–123, St. Julians, Malta. Association for Computational Linguistics.

Bloom Kenneth, Stein Sterling, and Shlomo Argamon. 2007. Appraisal extraction for news opinion analysis at ntcir-6.

Christopher Khoo, Armineh Nourbakhsh, and Jin-Cheon Na. 2012. Sentiment analysis of online news text: A case study of appraisal theory. *Online Information Review*, 36.

Guohao Li, Hasan Hammoud, Hani Itani, Dmitrii Khizbullin, and Bernard Ghanem. 2023. Camel: Communicative agents for "mind" exploration of large language model society. In *Advances in Neural Information Processing Systems*, volume 36, pages 51991–52008. Curran Associates, Inc.

James R. Martin and Peter R. White. 2005. *The language of evaluation: Appraisal in English.* Palgrave Macmillan.

Damilola Omitaomu, Shabnam Tafreshi, Tingting Liu, Sven Buechel, Chris Callison-Burch, Johannes Eichstaedt, Lyle Ungar, and João Sedoc. 2022. Empathic conversations: A multi-level dataset of contextualized conversations. *Preprint*, arXiv:2205.12698.

Isabella Poggi and D'Errico Francesca. 2010. Cognitive modelling of human social signals. In *Proceedings of the 2nd International Workshop on Social Signal Processing*, SSPW '10, page 21–26, New York, NY, USA. Association for Computing Machinery.

Jessica Sheringham, Isla Kuhn, and Jenni Burt. 2021. The use of experimental vignette studies to identify drivers of variations in the delivery of health care: a scoping review. *BMC Medical Research Methodology*, 21(1).

Jon Veloski, Stephen Tai, Adam S. Evans, and David B. Nash. 2005. Clinical vignette-based surveys: A tool for assessing physician practice variation. *American Journal of Medical Quality*, 20(3):151–157.

Xuewei Wang, Weiyan Shi, Richard Kim, Yoojung Oh, Sijia Yang, Jingwen Zhang, and Zhou Yu. 2019. Persuasion for good: Towards a personalized persuasive dialogue system for social good. In *Proceedings of the 57th Annual Meeting of the Association for Computational Linguistics*, pages 5635–5649, Florence, Italy. Association for Computational Linguistics.

Casey Whitelaw, Navendu Garg, and Shlomo Argamon. 2005. Using appraisal groups for sentiment analysis. In *Proceedings of the 14th ACM International Conference on Information and Knowledge Management*, CIKM '05, page 625–631, New York, NY, USA. Association for Computing Machinery.

Ludwig Wittgenstein. 1922. Tractatus logico-philosophicus. *Filosoficky Casopis*, 52:336–341.

Chengxing Xie, Canyu Chen, Feiran Jia, Ziyu Ye, Kai Shu, Adel Bibi, Ziniu Hu, Philip H.S. Torr, Bernard Ghanem, and G. Li. 2024. Can large language model agents simulate human trust behaviors? *ArXiv*, abs/2402.04559.

Xuhui Zhou, Hao Zhu, Leena Mathur, Ruohong Zhang, Haofei Yu, Zhengyang Qi, Louis-Philippe Morency, Yonatan Bisk, Daniel Fried, Graham Neubig, and Maarten Sap. 2024. SOTOPIA: Interactive evaluation for social intelligence in language agents. In *The Twelfth International Conference on Learning Representations*.

7 Appendix

7.1 Detailed Results for Insight

7.1.1 Factor Analysis

A varimax rotation factor analysis identifies distinct factors for the Insight of both GPT-3.5 and GPT-4, focusing on the Empath metrics: Optimism, Admire, Criticise, Worthwhile, and Negligible. We refer to these identified factors as "Insight Factors".

GPT-3.5: Each Empath metric loads onto a unique factor with a consistent factor loading of around .71.

GPT-4: Admire, Criticise, and Optimism independently load onto separate factors with similar loadings of .71. Worthwhile and Negligible share a factor. Worthwhile also loads onto another separate factor. To maintain clarity, we exclude Worthwhile from further analysis.

7.1.2 ANOVA Results

The ANOVA model includes Persona, Affect, Judgment, Appreciation, Model (GPT-3.5, GPT-4), and Insight Factors as independent variables, with the scores of the Insight Factors as the dependent variables. This model explains 59% of the variance in the data.

Affect and Insight Factors Interaction: The interaction is significant (F(3,23999) = 3314.8, p < .0001). Positive Affect increases Optimism scores, decreases Admire and Criticise scores, and reduces Negligible scores. There is a significant 3-way interaction between model-Affect-Factors, indicating that both models show the same patterns for how positive Affect impacts Optimism, Admire, and Criticise. However, GPT-3.5 uniquely demonstrates that positive Affect decreases Negligible scores.

Judgment and Insight Factors Interaction: The interaction proves significant (F(3,23999) = 1195.0, p < .0001). Positive Judgment leads to increased scores for Optimism and Admire, while it reduces those for Criticise and Negligible. The significant 3-way interaction between model-Judgment-Factors shows that these effects of positive Judgment remain consistent across both models, though there is a variation in how each model ranks these Factors in terms of their magnitude.

Appreciation and Insight Factors Interaction: The interaction is significant (F(3,23999) = 344.6, p < .0001). Positive Appreciation increases Optimism scores, reduces Admire and Negligible scores, but does not impact Criticise scores. The significant 3-way interaction between model-Appreciation-Factors indicates that the effects of positive Appreciation are similar across models, except that Admire scores in GPT-4 remain unaffected.

Persona Impact: No significant interactions are found between signal variables and Persona concerning Appreciation or Judgment. However, for Affect, significant interactions occur. The influence of positive versus negative Affect remains consistent within each Persona, though the intensity of the effect varies between positive and negative signals across different personas. Despite these variations, the overall impact on each persona remains unchanged.

7.2 Detailed Results for Response

7.2.1 Factor Analysis

The factor analysis indicates clearer separation for GPT-3.5 Response compared to that of GPT-4, with four out of five factors having high loadings ($\geq$ .9). GPT-4 Response shows more overlap between factors. Based on these findings, we focus on Emotional_Intensity, Emotional_Polarity/negative_Optimism, Empathy, Admire, and Criticise. Worthwhile is excluded due to its overlap with Emotional_Polarity/negative_Optimism in GPT-3.5 and with Admire in GPT-4. We also drop Negligible because of its inconsistent loadings across the two LLMs: it loads onto one factor for GPT-4 (with loading .54), but no factor for GPT-3.5. We refer to these identified factors as "Response Factors".

7.2.2 ANOVA Results

The ANOVA model includes Persona, Affect, Judgment, Appreciation, Model, and the five principal Response Factors identified in the factor analysis as independent variables, and the scores of these Response Factors as the dependent variables. The model explains 99% of the variance in the data.

Affect and Response Factors Interaction: This interaction is significant (F(4,2999) = 299.4, p < .0001). Negative Affect leads to increased empathy and polarity/negative_Optimism, while not affecting other response variables. There is a notable 3-way interaction between model-Affect-Factors, where both models demonstrate the same trends for empathy and polarity, but they react differently in terms of intensity: GPT-3.5 shows an increase in intensity in response to negative Affect, whereas GPT-4 shows a decrease.

Judgment and Response Factors Interaction: The interaction is significant (F(4,2999) = 70.5, p < .0001). Positive Judgment increases both empathy and intensity without affecting other variables. A marginal 3-way interaction between model-Judgment-Factors shows that while the absolute levels of empathy and intensity may vary between models, the relative increase in these Factors due to Positive Judgment remains consistent within each model. This suggests that regardless of the model, Positive Judgment reliably enhances both empathy and intensity.

Appreciation and Response Factors Interaction: The interaction is significant (F(4,2999) = 51.3, p < .0001). Positive Appreciation increases empathy and intensity without affecting other variables. The 3-way interaction between model-Appreciation-Factors indicates that while the specific values of empathy may vary, the differential impact of Positive versus Negative Appreciation on empathy does not vary within each model. Similarly, the effect on intensity is consistently positive across all models, indicating a stable response to Positive Appreciation.

Persona Impact: No significant interactions are found between signal variables and Persona, indicating consistent response patterns across different personas.

LLM	Empath	Affect Positive	Affect Negative	Judgment Positive	Judgment Negative	Appreciation Positive	Appreciation Negative	Persona counselor	Persona artist	Persona leader
GPT3.5	optimism	**0.07±0.03**	0.05±0.03	0.06±0.03	0.06±0.03	0.06±0.03	0.06±0.03	0.06±0.03	0.06±0.03	0.06±0.03
GPT3.5	admire	0.0±0.01	0.01±0.02	0.01±0.01	0.01±0.01	0.01±0.01	0.01±0.01	0.01±0.01	0.0±0.01	0.01±0.01
GPT3.5	criticise	0.0±0.0	0.0±0.0	0.0±0.0	0.0±0.0	0.0±0.0	0.0±0.0	0.0±0.0	0.0±0.0	0.0±0.0
GPT3.5	worthwhile	0.04±0.03	0.04±0.03	0.04±0.03	0.04±0.03	0.04±0.03	0.04±0.03	0.05±0.03	0.04±0.03	0.03±0.03
GPT3.5	negligible	0.0±0.0	0.0±0.0	0.0±0.0	0.0±0.0	0.0±0.0	0.0±0.0	0.0±0.0	0.0±0.0	0.0±0.0
GPT4	optimism	0.06±0.03	0.02±0.02	0.04±0.03	0.04±0.03	0.04±0.03	0.04±0.03	0.04±0.03	0.05±0.03	0.03±0.02
GPT4	admire	0.01±0.01	0.01±0.01	0.01±0.01	0.01±0.01	0.01±0.01	0.01±0.01	0.01±0.02	0.0±0.01	0.01±0.01
GPT4	criticise	0.0±0.0	0.0±0.0	0.0±0.0	0.0±0.0	0.0±0.0	0.0±0.0	0.0±0.0	0.0±0.0	0.0±0.0
GPT4	worthwhile	0.04±0.02	0.03±0.02	0.04±0.02	0.03±0.02	0.04±0.02	0.04±0.02	0.04±0.03	0.04±0.02	0.04±0.02
GPT4	negligible	0.0±0.0	0.0±0.0	0.0±0.0	0.0±0.0	0.0±0.0	0.0±0.0	0.0±0.0	0.0±0.0	0.0±0.0

Table 5: Mean and standard deviation of Empath topic scores (Optimism, Admire, Criticise, Worthwhile, Negligible) for the Response of the LLMs.

Name	Age	Occupation	Personality	Openness	Conscientiousness	Extraversion	Agreeableness	Neuroticism
Maria	45	High school counselor	empathetic, sociable	high	low	low	high	high
Alex	60	Tech entrepreneur	ambitious, assertive	high	high	high	low	low
Lily	25	Artist	adventurous, creative	high	low	high	high	low

Table 6: Detailed information of the three personas including name, age, occupation, personality, and the Big-Five personality traits (OCEAN).

Persona: Lily, a 25-year-old adventurous, creative artist

Input utterance (with positive Affect, positive Judgment, positive Appreciation):

Hi, I'm Pat. Please donate to our charity organization. Seeing the community come together in such a wonderful way gives us hope! Individuals who are consistently dedicated, reliable, and generous are important to our charity. Every penny you contribute is meaningful, fueling groundbreaking endeavors for so many children.

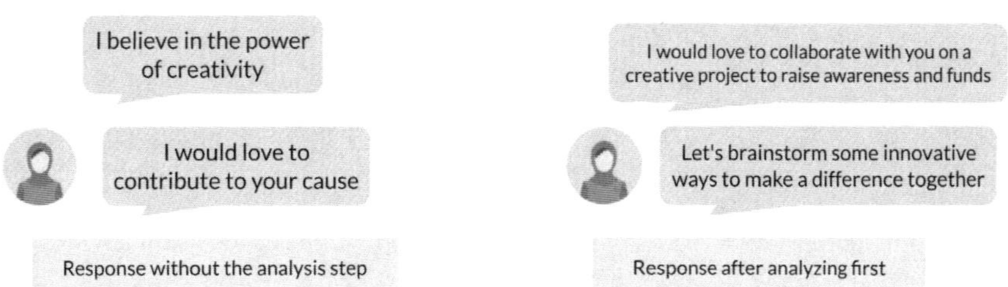

Figure 4: Comparison between the Responses of GPT-3.5 given persona Lily, without (left) and with (right) analysing the input utterance before generating the Response.

LLM	Social Signal	Empath	Cohen's d Effect Size
GPT3.5	Affect	optimism	**2.53**
		negligible	-1.0
	Judgment	admire	**1.0**
		criticise	**-1.41**
		negligible	-1.0
	Appreciation	negligible	**-1.41**
GPT4	Affect	optimism	**1.26**
	Judgment	admire	**1.0**
		criticise	**-1.41**
	Appreciation	worthwhile	**1.0**

Table 7: Values of Cohen' d that indicate large effect sizes for the generated Insight. We compute Cohen' d effective sizes for each social signal, each Empath category, and each model.

LLM	Social Signal	Social Intelligence Dimension	Cohen's d Effect Size
GPT3.5	Affect	empathy	-1.04
		emotional polarity	-0.92
GPT4	Affect	empathy	-1.21

Table 8: Values of Cohen' d that indicate large effect sizes for the generated Response. We compute Cohen' d effective sizes for each social signal, each social intelligence dimension, and each model.

LLM	Output	Persona	Optimism	Admire	Criticise	Worthwhile	Negligible	Emotional Polarity	Emotional Intensity	Empathy
GPT3.5	Insight	counselor	0	0	0	0	0	-	-	-
		artist	0	0.04	0	0.04	0	-	-	-
		leader	0	0.04	0	0	0	-	-	-
GPT3.5	Response	counselor	0.06	0.06	0	0.09	0	0.191	2.663	2.749
		artist	0.03	0	0	0	0	0.059	2.565	2.524
		leader	0.08	0	0	0.04	0	0.121	2.522	2.460
GPT4	Insight	counselor	0.02	0.02	0	0.01	0	-	-	-
		artist	0.01	0.02	0	0.03	0.01	-	-	-
		leader	0.03	0.01	0	0.02	0	-	-	-
GPT4	Response	counselor	0.02	0.05	0	0.02	0	0.205	2.655	2.521
		artist	0.09	0	0	0	0	0.213	2.356	2.762
		leader	0.02	0.02	0	0.02	0	0.289	2.327	2.394

Table 9: Values of our output quantitative metrics on generated Insight and Response of the neutral utterance. The social intelligence dimensions (emotional polarity, emotional intensity, empathy) are applied only to Response.

Aligning to Adults Is Easy, Aligning to Children Is Hard: A Study of Linguistic Alignment in Dialogue Systems

Dorothea French, Sidney D'Mello, Katharina von der Wense
University of Colorado Boulder
Boulder, CO, 80309
Dorothea.French@colorado.edu

Abstract

During conversations, people align to one another over time, by using similar words, concepts, and syntax. This helps form a shared understanding of the conversational content and is associated with increased engagement and satisfaction. It also affects conversation outcomes: e.g., when talking to language learners, an *above* normal level of linguistic alignment of parents or language teachers is correlated with faster language acquisition. These benefits make human-like alignment an important property of dialogue systems, which has often been overlooked by the NLP community. In order to fill this gap, we ask: (RQ1) Due to the importance for engagement and satisfaction, to what degree do state-of-the-art dialogue systems align to adult users? (RQ2) With a potential application to child language acquisition in mind, do systems, similar to parents, show high levels of alignment during conversations with children? Our experiments show that ChatGPT aligns to adults at roughly human levels, while Llama2 shows elevated alignment. However, when responding to a child, both systems' alignment is below human levels.

1 Introduction

Conversation allows people to share information by creating a collective representation of the conversational context, achieved in part by linguistic alignment (Garrod and Pickering, 2004; Pickering and Ferreira, 2008): when two people are conversing, the content of their speech as well as how it is phrased prime the other person to respond in a certain way. This reduces the chance of misunderstandings, since the used words and phrasing already have an established shared meaning, and thus, makes communication more efficient and enjoyable (Garrod and Pickering, 2004).

Linguistic alignment is critical in a variety of conversations, even those between a human and a virtual agent: prioritizing alignment in responses makes conversation with chatbots more effortless and less frustrating for users (Spillner and Wenig, 2021). Nevertheless, alignment is often overlooked by the NLP community and has not yet been studied in the context of state-of-the-art dialogue systems, even though they are becoming increasingly omnipresent. To fill this gap, we first ask: **(RQ1) To what degree do two state-of-the-art dialogue systems – ChatGPT and Llama2 – align to users, and does their alignment compare to that typically seen between humans?**

	Context
MOT	Hm?
CHI	Where Mommy go?
MOT	Mommy went to the university this morning to get some books.
CHI	Where's Mommy's books?
	Response
MOT	They're in the hallway in a big bag.
GPT	Mommy will bring the books home this evening.
Llama2	Mommy left her books in the car.

Table 1: The final lines of a dialogue excerpt from the CHILDES dataset, with the parent's true response and our system-generated responses.

Linguistic alignment plays an even greater role in educational contexts, such as language learning: amongst other benefits, aligned and comprehensible input and output prime the speaker to use appropriate syntactic structures, they can receive implicit feedback with recasts immediately after an error, and they recognize what parts of their speech led to any misunderstandings and negotiate a re-phrasal (Gass et al., 1998). Additionally, parents or caregivers show an elevated level of alignment when talking to young children (Misiek et al., 2020), and their level of alignment predicts how well the child's language skills develop (Denby and Yurovsky, 2019). As dialogue systems are used more and more in language learning contexts,[1] we

[1]Examples are the language learning software Duolingo

Proceedings of the 1st Human-Centered Large Language Modeling Workshop, pages 81–87
August 15, 2024 ©2024 Association for Computational Linguistics

further ask: **(RQ2) To what degree do ChatGPT and Llama2 align to children (i.e. non-fluent speakers), and how does this level of alignment compare to a parent's?**

We conduct experiments on the Switchboard Dialogue Acts Corpus (SWDA), which consists of adult–adult conversations (for RQ1) (Stolcke et al., 2000), and on the CHILDES dataset (Macwhinney, 2000), which contains child–parent conversations (for RQ2). We generate responses with ChatGPT and Llama2 and calculate three types of alignment – syntactic, lexical, and semantic – for each of their responses. Our results show that ChatGPT's alignment levels approximate those of humans when participating in standard adult conversation, but are lower than human level when responding to a child. Llama2 aligns above human levels in conversations with adults, but below human levels during dialogue with children. Overall, our results indicate room for improvement with regards to the alignment levels of dialogue systems.

2 Related Work

Exploring Linguistic Alignment Linguistic alignment is a mechanism by which humans mimic their partners in conversation – from phonology, to syntax and semantics (Garrod and Pickering, 2004). This kind of repetition lightens the cognitive load of language production, as certain structures are already primed from previous usage. Alignment at multiple levels such as lexical and syntactic results in alignment of situation models, as language production, comprehension, and interactive production are all interwoven (Pickering and Garrod, 2013). Alignment contributes to the success of a variety of human interaction. From the workplace – employees who show elevated levels of alignment over time are more likely to remain in the company (Doyle et al., 2016) – to the language classroom or nursery (Denby and Yurovsky, 2019). In some cases, the alignment of task-specific vocabularies strongly correlates with conversation outcomes (Fusaroli et al., 2012). Alignment as a feature of communication is also critical in human-computer interaction. Lexical alignment affects human understanding of a conversational agent during live conversation (Srivastava et al., 2023). It also contributes towards decreasing user frustration and perceived task load when interacting with a dialogue system (Spillner and Wenig, 2021).

and EFL classroom (Amin, 2023).

	Context
A	Any jury's not going to disregard the evidence, you know.
B	Uh, that's true.
B	I, I, I think our judicial system is attorney welfare myself.
A	That may very well be.
	Response
B	I, I hold it in the utmost contempt.
GPT	It's definitely a possibility that needs to be looked into.
Llama2	Yeah, it's like, you know, they're just trying

Table 2: The final lines of a dialogue excerpt from the SWDA corpus, with gold and generated responses

Analysis of Dialogue Systems While common to use the automatic scoring methods of word overlap with a ground truth (such as BLEU (Papineni et al., 2002) or ROUGE (Lin, 2004)) or words embeddings to evaluate dialogue systems, these metrics do not correspond highly with human judgement (Liu et al., 2017). Other automatic metrics, such as context coherence – how well the response matches the context of the conversation (Xu et al., 2018) – can result in improved systems. Outside of automatic metrics, human evaluation is critical and can look at dimensions such as informativeness, grammatically, coherence as well as how human-like or engaging the system is (Finch and Choi, 2020). The downside of human evaluation, however, is time and cost.

3 Experimental Setup

3.1 Data

Switchboard Dialogue Acts Corpus Our first corpus is the Switchboard Dialogue Acts Corpus (SWDA), which consists of a series of phone conversations on a variety of topics (Stolcke et al., 2000). All dialogues are between adults, which allows us to assess model alignment with adults, i.e., fluent speakers of English (RQ1). We use all 1157 transcripts.

CHILDES We also experiment with the CHILDES dataset, which consists of conversations between caretakers and children (Macwhinney, 2000), to assess the models' alignment to children, i.e., language learners (RQ2). We use the 7721 transcripts from North American English speakers aged 24 to 42 months.

Data Preparation To prepare the data, first we extract relevant dialogue excerpts from each transcript: the final two lines – the target utterance and response – must come from different participants and each be at least 3 words long. We then randomly select 10,000 excerpts from each dataset. Each excerpt is 36 lines long, allowing for one target response and 35 turns of context – a length chosen to ensure ChatGPT's has enough context to work with, as described in Appendix A. For the CHILDES transcripts, the true responses averaged 7.1 words, and for SWDA they averaged 9.1.

3.2 Models and Baseline

ChatGPT and Llama2 The first state-of-the-art model we experiment with is ChatGPT, a generative pretrained transformer (Vaswani et al., 2017) from the GPT 3.5 family of language models released by OpenAI. These models are trained using reinforcement learning from human feedback (Ouyang et al., 2022). We compare ChatGPT 3.5 turbo to the 7B and 13B chat versions of Llama2, trained using publicly available sources and Reinforcement Learning with Human Feedback (Touvron et al., 2023).

Prompting In each prompt, we provide the most recent 35 utterances from the dialogue as context. We use the following prompt for RQ1 (adults): "System: *You are having a conversation with person* <A or B>. *Respond with a single line approximately* <True Length> *words long.* A: <Utterance>, B: <Utterance>, ..."

Similarly, we use the following prompt for RQ2 (children): "System: *You are a parent talking to a child. Predict the parent's next line as best you can, even with little context. Respond with a single line approximately* <True Length> *words long.* MOT: <Utterance>, CHI: <Utterance>, ..."

We request a reply with approximately the same number of words as the gold response, as both systems produced overly long responses in preliminary experiments. When using ChatGPT, we check the returned message for a set of keywords (including "AI," "language model," "context," and "clarify") that indicate the model fails to provide a response to the conversation, then regenerate up to five times if needed before moving on.

Baseline To estimate the amount of random alignment for each dataset, we shuffle the responses and randomly pair them with a dialogue context. We do this separately for the true and generated responses.

Response set	Syntactic	Lexical	Semantic
True	0.444	0.170	0.308
True Baseline	0.405	0.117	0.248
ChatGPT	0.443	0.151	0.340
ChatGPT Baseline	0.418	0.117	0.280
Llama2 13B	0.472	0.207	0.350
Llama2 13B Baseline	0.421	0.130	0.277
Llama2 7B	0.475	0.213	0.374
Llama2 7B Baseline	0.420	0.130	0.286

Table 3: Alignment scores for the SWDA corpus

3.3 Alignment Metrics

We use the align package (Duran et al., 2019) to calculate syntactic, lexical, and semantic alignment. All are computed given the last (i.e., the most recent) context utterance u and the (true or generated) response r.

Syntactic Alignment To calculate the syntactic alignment a_{syn}, the utterance and response are segmented into uni-grams, tagged with part-of-speech (POS) information, and condensed into a set of unique POS tags with the counts of their occurrences: $u = (u_1, c_{u_1}), ..., (u_n, c_{u_n})$ and $r = (r_1, c_{r_1}), ..., (r_m, c_{r_m})$, with n and m being the number of unique POS tags in u and r, and c the number of times each tag occurs in the utterance. The syntactic alignment is then computed as the cosine similarity of the context and response vectors:

$$a_{syn} = \text{cosine}(v_u, v_r) \quad (1)$$

Lexical Alignment The process for lexical alignment a_{lex} is identical that of syntactic alignment, except using word lemmas instead of POS tags.

Semantic Alignment Lastly, semantic alignment a_{sem}, which describes how the utterance content overlaps, is calculated using word2vec embeddings (Mikolov et al., 2013) $e(u_1), ..., e(u_n)$ and $e(r_1), ..., e(r_m)$. We use a bag-of-words approach to obtain sentence representations e_u and e_r. Semantic alignment is computed as:

$$a_{sem} = \text{cosine}(e_u, e_r) \quad (2)$$

4 Results and Discussion

RQ1: Alignment to Adults All results for RQ1 are shown in Table 3. Comparing the alignment of ChatGPT to the true response, we see that there is less than 1% difference in the syntactic alignment, a 10% increase in semantic alignment, and a 12% decrease in lexical alignment. Semantic alignment is the only category in which ChatGPT

Response Set	Syntactic	Lexical	Semantic
True	0.490	0.278	0.411
True Baseline	0.359	0.069	0.181
ChatGPT	0.436	0.190	0.347
ChatGPT Baseline	0.367	0.071	0.196
Llama2 13B	0.464	0.227	0.345
Llama2 13B Baseline	0.371	0.073	0.179
Llama2 7B	0.473	0.251	0.370
Llama2 7B Baseline	0.366	0.075	0.180

Table 4: Alignment scores for CHILDES dialogues

overshoots human levels, which could indicate it is less likely to introduce new topics than a human. Both Llama models also show this trend. Llama2 overshoots human alignment in all categories – as the size of the Llama2 model decreases, so does its performance as it strays further from human-like alignment levels.

Turning to the baselines, for syntactic and lexical alignment, ChatGPT is closer to the randomized baseline than humans are; which means a higher fraction of its alignment does not come from matching a specific conversation, but from using more common words and syntax. The baseline alignments between all three models are fairly similar, although the semantic space of the smaller Llama2 model is less diverse as can be seen from a higher alignment baseline.

Upon manual inspection of 100 transcripts, we see that ChatGPT generates more convincing results. On a scale of 1 (makes minimal sense) to 5 (an ideal response) ChatGPT scored an average of 4.37. The responses are also much more likely to contain novel information or drive the conversation forward. However, it less convincingly mimics the style of the conversation and the human respondent. The Llama2 models both score below 3.50. They mimic stylistic elements, but oftentimes do not contribute positively to the conversation (i.e. generate responses such as "Oh, yeah!", "Uh-huh.", or duplicate the previous utterance). This shows that past a certain point, elevated levels of alignment may negatively correlate with response quality and sophistication.

RQ2: Alignment to Children Our results for RQ2 are shown in Table 4. First, we see that the syntactic alignment of ChatGPT is 12% lower than that of a human, lexical alignment is 37% lower, and semantic alignment is 17% lower. In contrast, Llama2 13B's alignments are 5%, 22%, and 19% lower, respectively. On one hand, these decreases might be due to difficulties understanding the conversation. The dialogues jump around and do not necessarily have a clear topical thread or goal. On the other hand, there is a divide in the metrics of success for a human parent and for a dialogue system – a parent does not need to successfully complete an inquiry or interaction, but needs to engage with the child in ways that further development (John et al., 2013). When comparing the levels of alignment of ChatGPT and Llama2 across datasets, we see syntactic and semantic change less than a few percent. Lexical alignment increases with CHILDES, perhaps due to a smaller inventory of words appearing in the context. Overall, we can conclude that the systems respond with a similar level of alignment regardless of the target audience.

Moreover, human-like alignment is not the only metric necessary to grade a model's quality. Inspection of the responses shows the ChatGPT responses are most convincing, at 3.86, although they show decrease in quality from the adult conversation. The Llama2 7b model averaged only 3.02, whereas the Llama2 13b model reached 3.35 – a smaller differential with ChatGPT than the adult conversation. When looking at what fraction of the responses were considered poor, 15% of the GPT responses to adults scored a 3 or less, whereas 26% of the responses to children were 3 or less. These were 41% and 63% respectively for the Llama 7b model, and 61% and 38% for the Llama 13b model. Overall, the quality of the Llama responses were below that of ChatGPT for children, and markedly lower for adults. Yet, when choosing a dialogue system to interact with children or language learners, Llama2 (or models that mimic conversation style more heavily) might still be a good choice: closer to human-like levels of alignment could aid in developing the child's language skills. This type of user might also care less about novelty and helpfulness of the system, and more about ease of understanding and lowered cognitive load.

5 Conclusion and Future Work

Dialogue systems show great potential to assist humans across a variety of tasks. The success of these interactions, like human–human interaction, correlates with linguistic alignment. Thus, we explore how state-of-the-art dialogue systems align to both adults and children. We find that, when responding to adult speakers, ChatGPT shows approximately human-level alignments and provides constructive responses. Llama2, however, overly mimics the conversation. This could be positive when talking with children or language learners as it results in heightened alignment. However, both models align below human levels. We conclude that SOTA dialogue systems have room for improvement in regards to reaching ideal levels of alignment under various circumstances.

In the future, we plan to investigate alignment to adult learners or non-typical speakers, in addition to exploring techniques to create dialogue systems with a closer-to-human level of alignment. We will also explore how well dialogue systems match the user in multi-turn conversational structures, and related outcomes (Fusaroli and Tylén, 2016).

Limitations

One of our primary limitations is that we are not able to use human participants to converse with the dialogue systems. While using existing datasets is an appropriate proxy to determine if this is an area which needs improvement, the chat systems may behave differently when dynamically adapting to a participant. Additionally, as we used commonly available data sets, there is a good chance they were part of the training data. Upon qualitative assessment of responses we did not find high similarity between the gold responses and generated responses for SWDA or CHILDES. Nonetheless, there is still a possibility the system has knowledge of the gold responses and used it when generating a reply – although in this case, the actual level of alignment would be lower than what we found, indicating our results are even more significant. In future works we would also like to explore using additional datasets and models. Lastly, while it does not directly affect the outcomes of this work, there is some ambiguity to the ideal level of alignment. We know that in many cases alignment correlates with positive outcomes, but it is a question for future work how much dialogue systems should be aligning to users and how variable that alignment should be across a variety of conversation types.

Ethics Statement

Our work analyzes current systems and suggests an avenue for future improvement. However, we do not intend to imply that dialogue systems should be used in all situations without additional consideration. Especially when interacting with children, we must ensure the accuracy of content and safety of communication methods. Additionally, while we point out a way in which state-of-the-art dialogue models exhibit below-human performance, the goal is not to make them more human-like as there is a lot of potential for harm when a chatbot cannot be distinguished from a person. Instead, we hope this work will help us improve dialogue systems as a tool and make them more useful in a variety of situations.

References

Momen Yaseen M. Amin. 2023. Ai and chat gpt in language teaching: Enhancing efl classroom support and transforming assessment techniques. *International Journal of Higher Education Pedagogies*, 4(4):1–15.

Joseph Denby and Daniel Yurovsky. 2019. Parents' linguistic alignment predicts children's language development. In *Annual Meeting of the Cognitive Science Society*.

Gabriel Doyle, Amir Goldberg, Sameer B Srivastava, Michael C Frank, et al. 2016. Alignment at work: Accommodation and enculturation in corporate communication. Technical report, Technical report.

Nicholas D. Duran, Alexandra Paxton, and Riccardo Fusaroli. 2019. Align: Analyzing linguistic interactions with generalizable techniques-a python library. *Psychological methods*.

Sarah E. Finch and Jinho D. Choi. 2020. Towards unified dialogue system evaluation: A comprehensive analysis of current evaluation protocols.

Riccardo Fusaroli, Bahador Bahrami, Karsten Olsen, Andreas Roepstorff, Geraint Rees, Chris Frith, and Kristian Tylén. 2012. Coming to terms: Quantifying the benefits of linguistic coordination. *Psychological Science*, 23(8):931–939.

Riccardo Fusaroli and Kristian Tylén. 2016. Investigating conversational dynamics: Interactive alignment, interpersonal synergy, and collective task performance. *Cognitive Science*, 40(1):145–171.

Simon Garrod and Martin Pickering. 2004. Why is conversation so easy? *Trends in Cognitive Sciences*, 8:8–11.

Susan M. Gass, Alison MacKey, and Teresa Pica. 1998. The role of input and interaction in second language acquisition: Introduction to the special issue. *The Modern Language Journal*, 82(3):299–307.

Aesha John, Amy Halliburton, and Jeremy Humphrey. 2013. Child–mother and child–father play interaction patterns with preschoolers. *Early Child Development and Care*, 183(3-4):483–497.

Chin-Yew Lin. 2004. ROUGE: A package for automatic evaluation of summaries. In *Text Summarization Branches Out*, pages 74–81, Barcelona, Spain. Association for Computational Linguistics.

Chia-Wei Liu, Ryan Lowe, Iulian V. Serban, Michael Noseworthy, Laurent Charlin, and Joelle Pineau. 2017. How not to evaluate your dialogue system: An empirical study of unsupervised evaluation metrics for dialogue response generation.

Brian Macwhinney. 2000. The childes project: tools for analyzing talk. *Child Language Teaching and Therapy*, 8.

Tomas Mikolov, Kai Chen, Greg Corrado, and Jeffrey Dean. 2013. Efficient estimation of word representations in vector space.

Thomas Misiek, Benoit Favre, and Abdellah Fourtassi. 2020. Development of multi-level linguistic alignment in child-adult conversations. In *Proceedings of the Workshop on Cognitive Modeling and Computational Linguistics*, pages 54–58, Online. Association for Computational Linguistics.

Long Ouyang, Jeff Wu, Xu Jiang, Diogo Almeida, Carroll L. Wainwright, Pamela Mishkin, Chong Zhang, Sandhini Agarwal, Katarina Slama, Alex Ray, John Schulman, Jacob Hilton, Fraser Kelton, Luke Miller, Maddie Simens, Amanda Askell, Peter Welinder, Paul Christiano, Jan Leike, and Ryan Lowe. 2022. Training language models to follow instructions with human feedback.

Kishore Papineni, Salim Roukos, Todd Ward, and Wei-Jing Zhu. 2002. Bleu: A method for automatic evaluation of machine translation. In *Proceedings of the 40th Annual Meeting on Association for Computational Linguistics*, ACL '02, page 311–318, USA. Association for Computational Linguistics.

Martin J. Pickering and Victor S. Ferreira. 2008. Structural priming: A critical review. *Psychological Bulletin*, 134(3):427–459.

Martin J. Pickering and Simon Garrod. 2013. An integrated theory of language production and comprehension. *Behavioral and Brain Sciences*, 36(4):329–347.

Laura Spillner and Nina Wenig. 2021. Talk to me on my level – linguistic alignment for chatbots. In *Proceedings of the 23rd International Conference on Mobile Human-Computer Interaction*, MobileHCI '21, New York, NY, USA. Association for Computing Machinery.

Sumit Srivastava, Mariët Theune, and Alejandro Catala. 2023. The role of lexical alignment in human understanding of explanations by conversational agents. In *Proceedings of the 28th International Conference on Intelligent User Interfaces*, IUI '23, page 423–435, New York, NY, USA. Association for Computing Machinery.

Andreas Stolcke, Klaus Ries, Noah Coccaro, Elizabeth Shriberg, Rebecca A. Bates, Daniel Jurafsky, Paul Taylor, Rachel Martin, Carol Van Ess-Dykema, and Marie Meteer. 2000. Dialogue act modeling for automatic tagging and recognition of conversational speech. *CoRR*, cs.CL/0006023.

Hugo Touvron, Louis Martin, Kevin Stone, Peter Albert, Amjad Almahairi, Yasmine Babaei, Nikolay Bashlykov, Soumya Batra, Prajjwal Bhargava, Shruti Bhosale, Dan Bikel, Lukas Blecher, Cristian Canton Ferrer, Moya Chen, Guillem Cucurull, David Esiobu, Jude Fernandes, Jeremy Fu, Wenyin Fu, Brian Fuller, Cynthia Gao, Vedanuj Goswami, Naman Goyal, Anthony Hartshorn, Saghar Hosseini, Rui Hou, Hakan Inan, Marcin Kardas, Viktor Kerkez, Madian Khabsa, Isabel Kloumann, Artem Korenev, Punit Singh Koura, Marie-Anne Lachaux, Thibaut Lavril, Jenya Lee, Diana Liskovich, Yinghai Lu, Yuning Mao, Xavier Martinet, Todor Mihaylov, Pushkar Mishra, Igor Molybog, Yixin Nie, Andrew Poulton, Jeremy Reizenstein, Rashi Rungta, Kalyan Saladi, Alan Schelten, Ruan Silva, Eric Michael Smith, Ranjan Subramanian, Xiaoqing Ellen Tan, Binh Tang, Ross Taylor, Adina Williams, Jian Xiang Kuan, Puxin Xu, Zheng Yan, Iliyan Zarov, Yuchen Zhang, Angela Fan, Melanie Kambadur, Sharan Narang, Aurelien Rodriguez, Robert Stojnic, Sergey Edunov, and Thomas Scialom. 2023. Llama 2: Open foundation and fine-tuned chat models.

Ashish Vaswani, Noam Shazeer, Niki Parmar, Jakob Uszkoreit, Llion Jones, Aidan N. Gomez, Lukasz Kaiser, and Illia Polosukhin. 2017. Attention is all you need.

Xinnuo Xu, Ondřej Dušek, Ioannis Konstas, and Verena Rieser. 2018. Better conversations by modeling, filtering, and optimizing for coherence and diversity. In *Proceedings of the 2018 Conference on Empirical Methods in Natural Language Processing*, pages 3981–3991, Brussels, Belgium. Association for Computational Linguistics.

A Context Length Selection

We want to choose a context length for the transcripts that maximizes the models' ability to responses accurately, while minimizing computing costs. We choose to use the CHIDLES dataset for this selection, as the transcripts with children on average were 100 words shorter than those with adults – this rules out the possibility that the models are simply not getting enough context. We primarily select based on ChatGPT's alignment levels, as it has higher computing costs and exhibited lower levels of alignment alongside more constructive responses .

A.1 Method

We randomly selected a subset of 200 transcripts with at least 101 turns to compare the effects of context length on ChatGPT's responses. The response is held constant, back-selecting increasing lengths of context.[2]

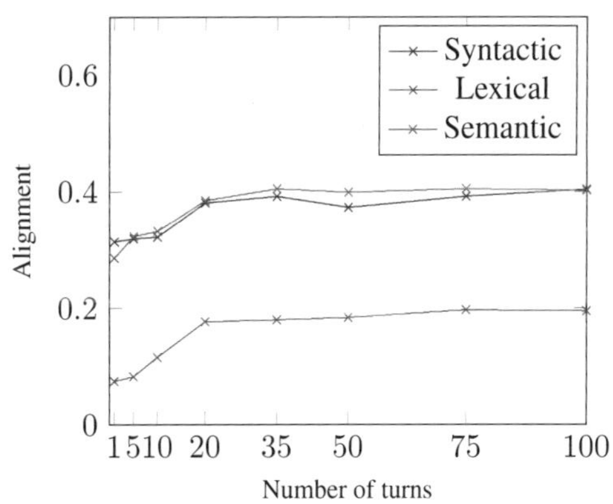

Figure 1: Alignment trends for ChatGPT's responses given varying context lengths

A.2 Decision

In these results, shown in Figure 1, we see a general trend in alignment for generated responses from different context lengths. The alignment in all three categories increases greatly up to 20 responses, and continue increasing slightly until 35 turns. We choose to use 35 turns to maximize ChatGPT's potential to provide a fully developed response while keeping computing costs manageable. While the adult transcripts generally have greater word counts, adding more context did not help ChatGPT generate better responses to the children, so we maintain keeping the number of turns constant across datasets. This selection of 35 turns does not imply an absolute requirement for length. Upon inspection, we see that in most cases the dialogue systems focus on the last few lines of context – allowing for the use of shorter transcipts if needed for other experiments.

[2]Additionally, we separately tried changing ChatGPT's temperature between 0 and 1, but only found minimal effects on alignment.

Author Index

Association for Computational Linguistics
209 N. Eighth Street
Stroudsburg, Pennsylvania 18360

ISBN 979-8-3313-0164-4

CURRAN ASSOCIATES INC.
proceedings.com